ASSESSMENT RESOURCES

McGRAW-HILL

SCIENCE

GRADES 3-6

McGraw-Hill School Division
New York Farmington

Table of Contents

Scope and Sequence of Process Skills in McGraw-Hill Science 

McGraw-Hill Science provides specific skill instruction.

- In Grades K–6: Each Unit provides Skill Builder activities that teach and practice Process Skills.
- In Grades K–2: Each Unit provides Science Builder activities, enabling skills which prepare children for higher level skills taught in Grades 3–6. (These are shaded in the boxes below.)

This table locates the Skill activity by **Unit (in bold type)** and Topic. White boxes are Skill Builders in the Pupil Edition. Shaded boxes are Science Builder Cards.

Skill	Kindergarten	Grade 1	Grade 2
Observe	**Learn About Your World,** Topic 1: Do you need light to see?	**A Tree,** Topic 1: Observe different parts of a plant.	**Watering Earth's Plants,** Topic 1: Use different senses to observe a plant.
Infer	**Make Things Move,** Topic 3: Why won't the toy work?	**The Sky,** Topic 1: Infer which place is warmer.	**Clues from the Past,** Topic 1: Infer what made the imprint.
Classify	**Learn About Animals,** Topic 1: How can you group pets?	**A Pond,** Topic 1: Find ways to classify pond animals.	**Rocky Homes,** Topic 1: Find ways to classify canyon animals.
Measure	**Weather and Seasons,** Topic 2: How can you measure how warm it is?	**Matter, Matter, Everywhere,** Topic 1: Measure your desk. your desk.	**Changes All Around,** Topic 1: Measure the temperature inside three cups. cups.
Use Numbers	**A Home Called Earth,** Topic 2: How many rocks are there?	**Being You,** Topic 1: Use numbers to show how you grow.	**Watch It Move,** Topic 1: Compare how much force it takes to move different objects.
Commun-icate	**Learn About Plants,** Topic 1: How can you show the plants growing? (draw)	**On the Move,** Topic 1: Use position words.	**Heart and Lungs,** Topic 1: Find and chart your pulse.

Skill	Kindergarten	Grade 1	Grade 2
Predict	**Learn About Your World:** Predict the next in a pattern. **Weather:** Predict based on previous knowledge; Based on what is observed.	**The Sky:** Tell what happens next in a pattern; Use a pattern to predict. **Matter, Matter, Everywhere:** Use the pattern to predict what happens next.	**Watering Earth's Plants:** Use flower pictures to make a pattern; Collect data and make a prediction. **Watch It Move:** Make predictions about a toy and ramp.
Interpret Data	**Learn About Your World:** Collect and organize facts. **Learn About Plants:** Make a picture. **Learn About Animals:** Read a picture. **Make Things Move:** Make a picture.	**A Tree:** Make a picture to show parts of a tree; Read a bar graph about how many trees. **A Pond:** Read a picture graph about geese; Find information about a pond.	**Clues from the Past:** Use a chart to compare animals; Collect and classify data; Get information from a diagram. **Changes All Around:** Organize data into a Chart; Read a bar graph. **Watch It Move:** Make a bar graph.
Form a Hypothesis	**A Home Called Earth:** Ask questions and name a problem based on what is observed.	**The Sky:** Ask questions about the Moon.	**Changes All Around:** Ask questions about sound.
Separate and Control (Use) Variables	**Make Things Move:** Identify things that can change results of an activity.	**On the Move:** Change something to make an object move farther.	**Rocky Homes:** Do two activities in which one thing is different.
Experiment	**Learn About Plants:** Follow directions in an activity.	**On the Move:** Follow directions to compare how objects move. **A Pond:** Decide if a test is fair.	**Watch It Move:** Follow directions to make a magnet.
Make a Model	**A Home Called Earth:** Choose objects that can be used as models.	**A Pond:** Make a model of a pond.	**Rocky Homes:** Make a model of how a rock changes.

Skill	Kindergarten	Grade 1	Grade 2
Define based on observa-tions	**Learn About Animals:** Identify what is done and observed in an activity.	**Matter, Matter, Everywhere:** Tell what happens in an activity.	**Rocky Homes:** Choose and make definitions about a canyon.
Recognize relation-ships (Grades K-2 only)	**Learn About Plants:** Make a sequence from a set of events.	**A Tree:** Use pictures to tell a story. **Matter, Matter Everywhere:** Make a pattern.	**Watering Earth's Plants:** Put events in order.

Each Skill Builder is followed up with practice and assessment in the Topic Review, Chapter Review, and Unit Review in which the Activity appears. Throughout each Unit, the featured skill trace is designated by this logo.

Grade 3	Grade 4	Grade 5	Grade 6
Where Living Things Live, Topic 5: Identifying Properties of an Environment	**Animals,** Topic 1: Observing Symmetry	**The Energy of Sound and Light,** Topic 6: Mixing Colors	**Heredity and Change,** Topic 6: Butterfly Adaptations
The Sun and Its Family, Topic 6: Using Observations to Explain an Event	**Matter on the Move,** Topic 2: Examine if Shape Affects Volume	**Ecosystems Around the World,** Topic 6: Comparing Ecosystems in Volcanic Areas	**Heredity and Change,** Topic 6: Butterfly Adaptations
Living Things, Topic 5: Comparing Living Things	**Classifying Living Things,** Topic 3: Classifying Leaves	**Plants,** Topic 5: Flowering Plants	**Cells, Growth, and Reproduction,** Topic 6: Comparing the Kingdoms
Rocks and Resources, Topic 4: Finding the Volume of a Water Sample	**A Body in Motion,** Topic 1: Measuring and Comparing Body Parts	**Pathways,** Topic 2: How Exercise Affects Your Heart and Lungs	**Response and Reproduction**, Topic 1: Reaction Time
Lift It, Push It, Pull It, Topic 2: Evaluating Differences	**Learning About Earth's History,** Topic 2: Comparing Sizes. **Electricity and Magnetism,** Topic 5: Numbers and Transformers	**Weather and Climate,** Topic 4: A Weather Station Model	**Properties of Matter and Energy,** Topic 3: Chemical Formulas. **Forces,** Topic 1: Speed. **Heredity and Change,** Topic 2: Finding Probability Using a Punnett Square

Grade 3	Grade 4	Grade 5	Grade 6
Matter and Energy, Topic 2: Making a Table	**Earth's Water,** Topic 1: Comparing Amounts of Water	**The Energy of Sound and Light,** Topic 2: Making Tables and Graphs	**Properties of Matter and Energy,** Topic 3: Chemical Formulas. **Response and Change,** Topic 3: Twins
The Sun and Its Family, Topic 2: Using Patterns	**Electricity and Magnetism,** Topic 3: Predict If It Will Light	**The Energy of Sound and Light,** Topic 6: Mixing Colors	**Forces,** Topic 1: Speed
Lift It, Push It, Pull It, Topic 2: Reading a Bar Graph. **Keeping Healthy,** Topic 3: Reading a Nutrition Label	**A Body in Motion,** Topic 3: Compare Smoke Now and in the Past	**Weather and Climate,** Topic 4: A Weather Station Model. **Ecosystems Around the World,** Topic 6: Comparing Ecosystems in Volcanic Areas	**The Restless Earth,** Topic 7: Half-Life
Rocks and Resources, Topic 2: How Weathered Materials Settle	**Animals,** Topic 6: How Do Adaptations Help an Animal Survive	**Earth and Its Resources,** Topic 6: How Do Wastes from Land Get into Lakes and Rivers? **Pathways,** Topic 2: How Does Exercise Affect Your Heart and Lungs?	**The Restless Earth,** Topic 1: What Makes the Crust Move?
Matter and Energy, Topic 5: Controlling an Experiment	**Earth's Water,** Topic 4: Surface Area and Evaporation	**Ecosystems Around the World,** Topic 1: Vanishing Bald Eagles	**Properties of Matter and Energy,** Topic 4: Which Warms Faster—Water or Sand?
World of Living Things, Topic 1: Observe How a Sow Bug Responds	**Matter on the Move,** Topic 4: How Heat Affects Evaporation	**Plants,** Topic 3: How Leaves Change Color. **Matter,** Topic 5: How Rusting Can Be Prevented	**Astronomy,** Topic 4: Paths in Space. **Response and Reproduction,** Topic 1: Reaction Time

Grade 3	Grade 4	Grade 5	Grade 6
Keeping Healthy, Topic 2: Germs and Antibodies	**Classifying Living Things,** Topic 2: Modeling Plant and Animal Cells	**Weather and Climate,** Topic 7: Climates in Two Areas. **Matter,** Topic 1: How Metal Boats Float. **Pathways,** Topic 3: How Do Your Kidneys Work?	**Cells, Growth, and Reproduction,** Topic 2: Cells—With or Without a Nucleus. **Astronomy,** Topic 3: A Model of the Tides. **Response and Change,** Topic 3: Twins
Where Living Things Live, Topic 1: A Forest Community	**Learning About Earth's History,** Topic 3: Defining the Flow of a Glacier	**Earth and Its Resources,** Topic 4: What Is Soil?	**Forces,** Topic 5: Double Levers

Introduction: To the Teacher

The McGraw-Hill *Science 2000* assessment program was designed to provide feedback to students, parents, teachers, and school administrators on the effectiveness of science instruction. McGraw-Hill's integrated assessment program provides students with feedback on how well they are achieving the instructional goals of the teacher and the expectations of their parents. Teachers receive feedback on how successfully Lesson Objectives and curriculum goals are being met and how well students are learning in different situations.

McGraw-Hill's traditional, alternative, and informal assessment options can:

- provide information about student performance in order to improve student learning.
- gauge how well students comprehend, communicate, and apply science knowledge.
- identify which students are in need of additional help, remediation, and reinforcement.
- provide students with an opportunity to demonstrate their talents and abilities.
- provide students with self-evaluation strategies to assess their own progress.

To be effective, McGraw-Hill believes that a science assessment program should

- **be varied and flexible,** coming in multiple formats.
- **be relevant and developmentally appropriate.**
- **be authentic** and grounded in the student's own educational experiences.
- **include many branches of the curriculum.** Science assessment should incorporate math, language arts, health, social studies, and the fine arts.
- give students an **opportunity to speak and write** using the language and concepts they have learned.
- **allow for diverse learning styles.** Science assessment should accommodate visual, auditory, spatial, logical/mathematical, and musical/rhythmic learners.
- **be frequent and ongoing.** In addition to assessment at the ends of Topics, Chapters, and Units, science assessment should include multiple opportunities for daily assessment throughout a lesson.
- **be aligned with the curriculum.** Questions and tasks should reflect specific objectives and course goals.

McGraw-Hill's *Science 2000* assessment program fulfills all these directives and encourages students and teachers to focus on:

- **science concepts.**
- **process skills.**
- **thinking skills.**
- **the factual knowledge of science.**
- **the methods of science.**

Overview of Assessment Resources

The *Science Assessment Guide* was designed to help you utilize the comprehensive assessment resources in the McGraw-Hill *Science 2000* program. The guide describes a wide range of assessment options and provides practical suggestions and guidelines to help you implement a successful assessment program. The *Science Assessment Guide* also reviews the Science Process and Thinking skills which are developed throughout the *Science 2000* program. Practical information about test administration and test-taking strategies for students is also provided.

The Explore Activities, Quick Labs, Skill Builder Activities, and the *Science Journal* are all designed to develop science concepts identified in the Lesson Objectives and to cultivate science process and Thinking Skills. These resources are described in the section Investigation and Reflection.

The use of class discussion, graphic organizers, Topic Reviews, Chapter Reviews, and Unit Reviews is described in the section Review and Reinforcement. These resources can assess the depth of student learning and the effectiveness of instruction prior to formal assessment. They provide additional practice and review and can identify Lesson Objectives for which students need reteaching and reinforcement.

Individual assessment strategies and suggestions for their use are described in the section Assessment. The table below summarizes the traditional, alternative, and informal assessment resources that are integrated with the *Science 2000* program.

Overview of Science Assessment Resources

Component	Resource	Assessment Strategies Traditional	Alternative	Informal
Pupil Edition	Brain Power		✔	
	Chapter Review	✔	✔	
	Design Your Own Experiment		✔	
	Explore Box		✔	
	Explore Activity		✔	
	Inquiry		✔	
	National Geographic FUNtastic Facts	✔		
	Problems and Puzzles		✔	
	Quick Lab		✔	
	Reading Charts, Diagrams, and Graphs	✔	✔	
	Science Journal		✔	✔
	Skill Builder		✔	
	Topic Review	✔		✔
	Unit Review	✔	✔	✔
	Why It Matters		✔	✔
Teacher Edition	Alternative Explore Activity		✔	
Test Book	**Chapter Tests**	✔		
	Unit Tests	✔		
Teacher Assessment Resources	**Graphic Organizers**		✔	
	Performance Assessments		✔	
Science Assessment Guide	Alternative Assessment Suggestions		✔	
	Observation & Interview			✔
	Portfolio Assessment		✔	
	Self/Group Assessment		✔	✔
	Traditional Assessment Suggestions	✔		

Test Administration

Chapter and Unit Tests are designed to be administered on a regular basis as part of an ongoing assessment program. Traditional assessments should complement alternative and informal assessments in a varied and flexible assessment program. The Chapter and Unit Tests can help you determine which students need additional help and where classroom instruction needs to be modified.

Every three to five days, as the Lesson Cycle for each Chapter Topic is completed, have students complete the Review at the end of each Topic. Reteach as necessary. You may want to give a quiz over the Topic's concepts and Science Words at this time to check for students' comprehension and understanding.

At the conclusion of a Chapter, have students complete the Chapter Review for practice and reinforcement. The Chapter Review prepares students for the Chapter Test and checks for comprehension and understanding. Chapter Test Form A can be administered as a practice test; Test Form B can then serve as the formal Chapter Test. As an alternative, Chapter Test A can be administered as a formal test. Chapter Test B can then be given to students who were absent, or to students who need to retake the Chapter Test after additional reteaching and review. Chapter Test B can also be used for additional practice and review to prepare students for a Unit Test. The latter strategy is helpful when reviewing the first Chapter in a Unit after students have completed the second Chapter.

The Unit Review should be completed at the conclusion of a Unit. The purpose of the Unit Review is to:

- help unify important science concepts and vocabulary.
- develop Science Process and Thinking Skills.
- provide additional practice and reinforcement.
- check for comprehension and understanding.
- prepare students for the Unit Test.

Following the Unit Review, reteach as necessary before administering the Unit Test.

Science Process Skills

Science Process Skills are skills that students learn as they carry out scientific inquiry. Rather than a single scientific method, students employ a variety of Process Skills when they are actively involved in scientific investigation. The Process Skills for each Unit and the activities where they are emphasized can be found in the Suggested Daily Planner in the Chapter Organizer. The Process Skills are observing, classifying, inferring, predicting, communicating, measuring, using numbers, interpreting data, experimenting, controlling variables, hypothesizing, defining operationally, and formulating models.

Observing is using your senses. You observe by seeing, hearing, tasting, touching, and smelling. Some student behaviors done while observing are:

- using senses other than sight.
- organizing objects by a single property.
- identifying multiple properties.
- identifying changes in objects.
- making quantitative observations (example: "5 kilograms" instead of "heavy").
- making qualitative observations (example: "smells like sour milk" instead of "smells").

Classifying is grouping objects by properties. Some student behaviors are:

- identifying a common property (minerals that look like metals and minerals that do not).
- sorting using two or more properties (minerals with cleavage that can scratch glass; and minerals without cleavage and minerals with cleavage that cannot scratch glass).

Inferring is using what you observed to explain something that has happened. Inferring goes beyond an observation to interpret what has been observed. For example: You see a patch of dead grass. An inference you might make is that grub worms are present in the soil causing the grass to die. Some student behaviors done while inferring are:

- linking observations to prior experiences or knowledge.
- proposing explanations for observations.

Predicting is proposing possible outcomes of an experiment. Predictions are based on earlier observations and inferences. Predictions are statements about what a future observation might be, while inferences attempt to provide reasons why something happened. Some student behaviors are:

- using appropriate data and observations.
- interpreting data/graphs.

- making generalizations about patterns.
- verifying appropriate predictions.

Communicating is telling what you know by speaking, writing, drawing, demonstrating, or graphing. Some student behaviors done while communicating are:
- describing observations or explanations using appropriate vocabulary.
- developing graphs or drawings to represent observations and display data.
- designing posters or diagrams to present data to persuade others.

Measuring is finding the size of an object, how much an object holds, or how much space it takes up. The object is compared to a unit of measure such as a paper clip or a centimeter. This process is used for making quantitative observations. Some student behaviors are:
- measuring length, volume, mass, temperature, and time in appropriate units.
- selecting appropriate equipment and units for the specific measuring tasks.

Using Numbers includes ordering, counting, adding, subtracting, multiplying, and dividing numbers. Some student behaviors done while using numbers are:
- counting.
- sequencing.
- ordering numbers in correct patterns.
- using mathematical skills appropriately.

Interpreting Data is explaining the meaning of information that has been collected. Some student behaviors are:
- ordering data.
- recognizing patterns or relationships.
- making appropriate inferences using data.
- summarizing appropriately.

Experimenting is testing hypotheses or predictions. In an experiment, all variables must be kept the same except one. Some student behaviors done while experimenting are:
- making and testing predictions about events.
- proposing and testing hypotheses.
- identifying and controlling variables.
- evaluating predictions and hypotheses based upon experimental results.

Controlling Variables is making sure that everything in an experiment stays the same except for one factor. Some student behaviors are:
- identifying variables that affect outcomes.
- identifying variables that are changed in the experiment.
- identifying variables that are controlled in an experiment.

Hypothesizing is making a reasonable guess that can be tested about how or why something happens. Some student behaviors done while hypothesizing are:

- forming hypotheses based upon observations and inferences.
- designing ways to test hypotheses.
- revising hypotheses when data does not support the original hypotheses.

Defining Operationally is forming a definition that is based on what you do or what you observe. An operational definition tells how something acts, not what it is. Some student behaviors are:

- describing experiences using concrete objects.
- telling what objects do.
- describing changes or measurements during an event.

Formulating Models is constructing verbal, mental, or physical representations of ideas, objects, or events and using them to explain or demonstrate relationships. One example of student behavior:

- designing a model of Earth, the Moon, and the Sun to explain phases or eclipses.

See page 8 for Science Process Skills Checklist with scoring rubric.

Science Process Skills: Checklist and Rubric

STUDENT NAMES	Observing	Classifying	Inferring	Predicting	Communicating	Measuring	Using Numbers	Interpreting Data	Experimenting	Controlling Variables	Hypothesizing	Defining Operationally	Formulating Models

Scoring Rubric:	**4** = Excellent	**3** = Good	**2** = Fair	**1** = Poor

Using Methods of Science

This list is useful as a comprehensive assessment tool. It might be best be used to summarize observations recorded on more detailed checklists for individual activities. See the checklists for Explore Activities, Skill Builders, and so on. There will be some duplication between this comprehensive list and those more detailed checklists.

1. Safety and Responsibility
- Demonstrates safe practices in class and field activities
- Uses and conserves resources
- Disposes of materials safely

2. Plans and Prepares for Investigations
- Makes and states observations that lead to investigation
- Asks well-defined questions based on observations
- Forms a testable hypothesis
- Describes a valid test before starting an investigation
- Reads directions thoroughly before starting
- Selects appropriate tools, including technology as needed
- Identifies variables as needed

3. Data-Collecting Procedures
- Uses tools accurately
- Uses tools safely
- Shares tools with partners as needed
- Makes observations and measurements accurately
- Records information in well-constructed tables as needed
- Makes accurate, well-labeled drawings as needed
- Repeats tests as needed to increase reliability

4. Concludes and Analyzes
- Analyzes and interprets information to construct reasonable explanations
- Communicates valid conclusions in writing and discussion
- Uses and cites pertinent background materials, including texts and references books
- Constructs graphs, tables, maps, and charts as needed to organize, examine, and evaluate information and communicate conclusions
- Cites data that support or disagree with the hypothesis as needed
- States any additional hypotheses based on the test results

4-point Rubric

1 point per category above. For category 1, all items should be checked for a student to receive 1 point. In all other categories, all—or most, as determined by you—items that apply should be checked for a student to receive 1 point.

Explore Activities, Quick Labs, and Skill Builders

National curriculum reports in all content areas recommend more experiential hands-on learning. A strong theme in the National Science Education Standards is that learning science is an active process. A greater emphasis on guiding students in active and extended scientific inquiry is recommended. The Explore Activities, Quick Labs, and Skill Builders are designed to encourage students to "learn by doing." Each activity has writing and/or drawing prompts to integrate with the *Science Journal*. The activities can also be used for performance assessments. Many of them involve cooperative learning.

Each Chapter has one or more Explore Activities designed to integrate and reinforce Chapter Science Concepts and Science Process Skills with an open-ended, discovery-based activity. Each Chapter also has a Skill Builder page that reinforces one or two Science Process Skills which are clearly identified in the title. The Explore Activities and Skill Builders are organized into the sections **Materials, Procedures, Conclude and Apply,** and **Going Further.** Within each section, Critical Thinking Skills are identified by boldface uppercase letters.

Each Chapter has one or more Quick Lab boxes that develop a Topic science concept by integrating it with Science Process Skills. Each Quick Lab prompts students to develop a hypothesis. The Quick Labs are divided into the sections **Materials, Procedures,** and **Conclude and Apply.** Within each section, Critical Thinking skills are identified by boldface uppercase letters.

Explore Activity / Quick Lab: Checklist and Rubric

STUDENT NAMES	Forms a Testable Hypothesis	Follows Procedures	Uses Time Wisely	Uses Appropriate Materials	Follows Safety Guidelines	Records Observations	Organizes Data	Applies Science Concepts	Draws Conclusions	Contributes to Team (As Applicable)

Scoring Rubric:	**4** = Excellent	**3** = Good	**2** = Fair	**1** = Poor

Skill Builder: Checklist and Rubric

STUDENT NAMES	Lesson Goal Achievement	Skill Mastery	Adherence to Procedures	Completeness of Data	Organization of Data	Time Management	Appropriate Use of Materials	Observations and Data Analysis	Conclusions	Teamwork (As Applicable)

Scoring Rubric:	**4** = Excellent	**3** = Good	**2** = Fair	**1** = Poor

Investigation Skills

Skill	Skill Builders	Be a Scientist Glossary Terms/Explore Process Words	Other Program Elements
Gathers information	Observe Measure Experiment	Collect Data	Be a Scientist text
Analyzes information from direct and indirect sources	Infer Interpret Data Make a Model	Draw Conclusions Compare and Contrast	Be a Scientist text
Analyzes information with logic and objectivity	Use Numbers Interpret Data	Draw Conclusions Make Decisions Compare Compare and Contrast Cause and Effect Sequence	Be a Scientist text
Constructs graphic organizers to evaluate and organize information	Communicate		Be a Scientist text
Identifies patterns and relationships	Observe Classify Infer Use Numbers Predict Interpret Data Use Variables Experiment	Compare Compare and Contrast Cause and Effect Sequence Identify Patterns (Grades 5/6)	Be a Scientist text
Constructs reasonable explanations	Infer Form a Hypothesis Experiment Make a Model Define Terms Based on Observations	Draw Conclusions Cause and Effect	Be a Scientist text
Formulates valid conclusions	Interpret Data Experiment	Draw Conclusions Cause and Effect	Be a Scientist text
Uses appropriate equipment and technology	Measure Experiment	Plan Collect Data Make Decisions	Be a Scientist text Handbook
Practices science safety rules		Make Decisions	Be a Scientist text Handbook
Analyzes scientific explanations: strengths vs. weaknesses		Analyze Evaluate	Be a Scientist text Science Magazines (Discussion Starter) History of Science Annotations
Evaluates the impact of research on scientific thought, society, and environment		Analyze Evaluate	Be a Scientist text Science Magazines (Discussion Starter) History of Science Annotations

Investigation Skills: Checklist and Rubric

STUDENT NAMES	Gathers Information	Analyzes Information from Direct and Indirect Sources	Analyzes Information with Logic and Objectivity	Constructs Graphic Organizers to Evaluate and Organize Information	Identifies Patterns and Relationships	Constructs Reasonable Explanations	Formulates Valid Conclusions	Uses Appropriate Equipment and Technology	Practices Science Safety Rules	Analyzes Scientific Explanations: Strengths vs. Weaknesses	Evaluates the Impact of Research on Scientific Thought, Society, and the Environment

Scoring Rubric: **4** = Excellent **3** = Good **2** = Fair **1** = Poor

Scientific Reasoning Skills

Skill	Skill Builders	Be a Scientist Glossary Terms/Explore Process Words	Other Program Elements
Longing to know and understand	Observe Experiment	Ask Questions	Be a Scientist text
Questioning of scientific assumptions		Ask Questionse Analyze Evaluate	Be a Scientist text History of Science Annotations Science Magazine (Discussion Starter)
Search for data and its meaning	Classify Infer Measure Use Numbers Interpret Data Experiment Make a Model Define Terms Based on Observations	Ask Questions Plan Collect Data Compare Identify Compare and Contrast Analyze Evaluate Identify Patterns (Grades 5 and 6)	Be a Scientist text
Demand for verification	Use Numbers Experiment Interpret Data	Repeat	Be a Scientist text
Respect for logic	Classify Infer Predict Interpret Data Use Variables Define Terms Based on Observations	Plan Draw Conclusions Cause and Effect Sequence Analyze Evaluate Identify Patterns (Grades 5 and 6)	Be a Scientist text
Consideration of premises	Infer Predict Form a Hypothesis Use Variables Experiment	Plan Cause and Effect	Be a Scientist text
Consideration of consequences	Infer Predict Interpret Data Use Variables Experiment	Draw Conclusions Cause and Effect Sequence Analyze Evaluate Identify Patterns (Grades 5 and 6)	Be a Scientist text
Respect for historical consequences			Be a Scientist text Science Magazines (Discussion Starter) History of Science Annotations

Scientific Reasoning Skills: Checklist and Rubric

STUDENT NAMES	Longing to know and understand	Questioning of scientific assumptions	Search for data and its meaning	Demand for verification	Respect for logic	Consideration of premises	Consideration of consequences	Respect for historical consequences

Scoring Rubric:	**4** = Excellent	**3** = Good	**2** = Fair	**1** = Poor

Using the *Science Journal*

A **journal** is an alternative assessment based on a written record of a student's thoughts about the subject matter he or she is studying. Journal entries are usually informal, personal, spontaneous, and exploratory in nature. Journal writing actively involves students in their own learning. Through the use of broad, open-ended questions and writing prompts, students are encouraged to pursue ideas, conduct thought experiments, engage in speculation, analyze, and synthesize. Journals can help students focus their thoughts, reflect on new ideas and concepts, and make connections to prior knowledge.

The *Science Journal* provides a place for students to write down their questions, ideas, reactions, thoughts, reflections, predictions, and observations. Because student entries in the *Science Journal* are intended to promote higher-order thinking, they should not be graded for spelling and grammar. A student's journal entries should open a private channel of communication between you and that student in a low-risk setting. They provide a daily record of student performance, growth, and personal development. The *Science Journal* helps students make a connection between science theory and their own experiences. It provides insight into their understanding of how science relates to the everyday world.

Questions and writing prompts for the *Science Journal* are found in the Skill Builder pages, the Explore Activity pages and boxes, and the Quick Lab boxes. Encourage students to include drawings, graphic organizers, and other forms of communication in their *Science Journals.* A *Science Journal* can also be used as part of a student's portfolio.

Class Discussion

Class discussion is a powerful technique to introduce, teach, and review science concepts. Frequent class discussion can be used to:

- actively engage and focus students.
- increase student interest and participation.
- give students an opportunity to speak using the language and concepts they have learned.
- assess the depth of prior knowledge.
- identify misconceptions.
- develop the language of science in context.
- check for comprehension and understanding.
- develop and reinforce communication skills.
- informally assess student learning.

There are many opportunities to pose questions and initiate class discussion in the Pupil and Teacher Editions.

Discussion Opportunities	Location	
Ask Questions	Daily Reading Skill box	TE
Ask Students	Language Support box	TE
Ask Students	Teach Cycle of Lesson	TE
Build on Prior Knowledge Questions	Introduce Cycle of Lesson	TE
Discussion Prompt	Reading Charts, Diagrams, and Graphs box	PE
Discussion Starter	Teach Cycle of Lesson	TE
Explore Question	Explore box	TE
FUNtastic Fact Questions	National Geographic box	PE
Lesson Objective Questions	Close/Assess Cycle of Lesson	TE
Question-Style Headings	Lesson headings/titles	PE
Think About It Questions	Why It Matters (Topic Review)	PE
Warm-up Activity Questions	Warm-Up Activity box	TE

Topic Review

The Pupil Edition is divided into Units, Chapters, and Topics. In the Teacher Edition, Topics are divided into five Lessons. At the conclusion of each Topic, students are presented with review questions that develop Science Process and Thinking Skills. **Why It Matters** questions offer students opportunities for discussion and writing. Selected Topic reviews also contain writing prompts to develop the Chapter Reading Skill. The end of Topic questions are aligned with the Lesson Objectives in the Teacher Edition.

Chapter Review

The end-of-Chapter Reviews are divided into four sections. **Using Science Words** reviews student understanding of the science vocabulary. **Understanding Science Ideas** assesses student comprehension of important science concepts that are developed throughout the Chapter. **Using Ideas and Skills** assesses a student's ability to apply scientific knowledge to answer questions or solve problems. **Problems and Puzzles** presents students with a performance opportunity. Chapter Review questions assess specific Science Process and Thinking skills which are identified in boldface type. Chapter Review questions are also aligned with the Lesson Objectives in the Teacher Edition. Chapter Tests, Chapter Reviews, and Unit Reviews all have the same format and organization.

Unit Review

Each Unit Review is divided into seven sections that utilize traditional, alternative, and informal assessment strategies:

Section 1 **Using Science Words** reviews student understanding of the Unit's science vocabulary. (fill-in-the blank)

Section 2 **Understanding Science Ideas** assesses student comprehension of important science concepts that are developed throughout the Unit. (multiple choice)

Section 3 **Using Ideas and Skills** assesses a student's ability to apply scientific knowledge to answer a question or solve a problem. (extended response)

Section 4 **Thinking Like a Scientist** asks the student to extend their scientific knowledge to a new situation. (extended response)

Section 5 **Writing in Your Journal** uses writing prompts that ask students to apply scientific knowledge to a new situation. (extended response, performance task)

Section 6 **Design Your Own Experiment** develops the Science Process Skills of Experimenting and Controlling Variables. (performance task)

Section 7 **Problems and Puzzles** are writing prompts and performance tasks that develop and extend science concepts and skills.

Unit Review questions assess specific Science Process and Thinking Skills which are identified in boldface type. The questions are also aligned with the Lesson Objectives in the Teacher Edition.

Graphic Organizers

Graphic organizers are graphical representations of written and verbal statements. Graphic organizers help students visualize associations, connections, and relationships. They provide a conceptual framework for students to collect and categorize ideas. Graphic organizers are powerful thinking tools that help students:

- organize information they gather during reading, listening, and viewing.
- organize the thoughts they generate for writing and speaking.
- recognize relationships and connections that exist among words and concepts.
- comprehend, summarize, and synthesize complex ideas.

Using graphic organizers allows students to identify key concepts and relate them to prior knowledge. Graphic organizers can also be used to detect missing information, identify misconceptions, and clarify relationships. Graphic organizers can often communicate ideas with more impact and visual clarity than text passages. Using graphic organizers promotes Science Process Skills by presenting opportunities for analysis that reading alone cannot provide.

As you use graphic organizers to enhance teaching and learning and for review and reinforcement, remind students that the graphic organizers you show them are only examples. Encourage students to make up their own webs, charts, and diagrams. Many of the Reading Graphs and Reading Diagrams boxes are linked to graphic organizers or ask students to construct a graphic organizer.

Examples of graphic organizers include flow charts, spider maps, compare/contrast matrices, fishbone maps, pie charts, cluster diagrams, cycle diagrams, classification/organization charts, Venn diagrams, time lines and continuum scales, concept maps, series of events chain, etc.

Traditional Assessment

Traditional assessment uses both conventional extended-response questions and traditional closed questions, such as multiple choice, true or false, fill in the blank, and matching, on standardized tests. Extended-response questions are assessment items that ask students to provide written explanations, drawings, or diagrams. Closed questions are objective assessment items in which a correct answer is not open to interpretation.

The twenty-eight Chapter and seven Unit tests in the Test Book complement the content and organization of the Chapter and Unit Reviews in the Pupil Edition. The test questions are also aligned with the Lesson Objectives in the Teacher Edition. The traditional test cycle measures student acquisition and retention of scientific knowledge and measures their ability to apply what they have learned to objective and extended-response questions. McGraw-Hill's traditional test materials are designed to assess student:

- comprehension of Science Words.
- understanding of science concepts and Lesson Objectives.
- Science Process and Thinking skills.
- ability to analyze information and solve problems.
- ability to apply scientific knowledge to new situations.

Chapter Tests

Each Chapter Test is designed to measure student comprehension of science concepts that are developed over several related Topics. The Test Book includes two Chapter tests for each Chapter—Test Form A and Test Form B. Using both tests will assess all the Chapter Objectives. The Chapter Objectives are identified in the Teacher Edition at the beginning of each Lesson cycle and in the Suggested Daily Planner for each Chapter. Each two-page test has ten questions. The test format includes fill-in-the-blank, multiple-choice, and extended-response questions.

Each test is divided into three sections. The section **Using Science Words** assesses student understanding of the Science Words which are identified at the beginning of each topic and in boldfaced type throughout the Chapter. The section **Understanding Science Ideas** assesses student comprehension of important science concepts that are developed throughout the Chapter. The section **Using Ideas and Skills** assesses student ability to apply scientific knowledge to answer a question or solve a problem. Questions in this section assess specific Science Process and Thinking Skills which are identified in boldface type. Every Chapter Test concludes with a Thinking Like a Scientist question which asks students to extend their scientific knowledge to a new situation.

Unit Tests

The seven Unit tests are designed to measure student comprehension of the science concepts that are developed over an entire Unit. Each Unit Test assesses the Lesson Objectives which are identified in the Teacher Edition at the beginning of each Lesson cycle and in the Suggested Daily Planner. Each four-page test contains 20 questions for grades 3 and 4, and 25 questions for grades 5 and 6.

Unit Tests use the same format as the Chapter Tests: fill-in-the-blank, multiple-choice, and extended-response questions. Each test is divided into three sections: **Using Science Words**, **Understanding Science Ideas**, and **Using Ideas and Skills**. Like Chapter Tests, Unit Tests assess the comprehension of science words and science concepts, the application of scientific knowledge, and Science Process and Thinking Skills. Every Unit Test concludes with a Thinking Like a Scientist question which asks students to extend their scientific knowledge to a new situation.

Performance Assessment

A **performance assessment** is an alternative assessment based on an open-ended task or hands-on activity designed to measure student performance against a specific set of criteria. Performance assessment tasks require students to draw upon a variety of skills, concepts, and knowledge. Performance assessments are not intended to test factual recall, but instead assess the application of factual knowledge and scientific concepts to a realistic problem or task. They ask students to explain the "why and how" of a concept or process. In performance assessment, students restructure factual information rather than just restating it. Performance assessments give students an opportunity to demonstrate their Science Process Skills, think logically, apply prior knowledge to a new situation, and identify novel solutions to a problem.

Performance assessments allow you to:

- evaluate how students apply scientific knowledge and Process Skills.
- check for the development of Critical Thinking Skills.
- assess student learning in realistic situations with different contexts.
- measure the depth of student understanding and insight.
- evaluate how persistent, imaginative, and creative students are when they approach tasks.

Performance assessment is an important component of authentic assessment. An authentic assessment measures student performance in a real-life task, relevant situation, or purposeful problem that is worthwhile, meaningful, and significant. This form of assessment often involves rich and complex ideas and materials. A performance task:

- actively engages the learner, increasing student interest and motivation.
- often does not have an easy approach to the task or a clear-cut solution to the problem.
- often asks students to conduct research or gather data. They may also be asked to estimate data.
- considers student ideas and opinions as important and credible components of the assessment.
- often requires students to make assumptions and decisions.
- may have several entry points that encourage students at different levels of understanding to begin working on the assessment.
- often includes situations which are open-ended and have multiple possibilities.
- often involves methods and results which are variable.
- usually requires presentation and communication skills.
- is usually more complex and experiential than a task in a traditional test.
- often models the kind of activity that takes place during science instruction.

Each Unit-by-Unit Performance Assessment Task includes student pages, a teacher page to help you administer the task, and a customized scoring rubric. Each Performance Assessment Task is aligned with one of the Science Process Skills which are reinforced in the Unit's Skill Builder pages. These performance tasks encourage students to demonstrate their ability to apply Science Process Skills to that Unit's concepts. They are open-ended to provide students with multiple opportunities for success. Many Performance Assessment Tasks involve teamwork, collaboration, and cooperative learning.

The Explore Activity pages, the Skill Builder page, and the Quick Lab boxes in each Chapter can be used as performance tasks.

The following suggestions may prove helpful when administering a performance task. Carefully review the instructions and expectations for the task. If appropriate, model the task or activity. Show examples of student work from previous years. Explain to the students how they will be evaluated. Review the scoring criteria on the rubric and justify the difference between an "excellent," "good," "fair," and "poor" performance. During the activity, you may wish to use the Science Process and Investigation Skills Checklists to record student proficiency as you observe them working on the task. After accessing and evaluating the performance tasks, you may wish to use student work to initiate a follow-up class discussion. Encourage students to share their ideas and approaches. If you have room, publish student work in the classroom.

Rubrics

A **rubric** is a set of scoring criteria used to evaluate student work and assess student performance. Rubrics are guidelines that are especially helpful in assessing the multidimensional aspects of a performance assessment. They can assist you in making distinctions that are more refined than simply identifying an answer as correct or incorrect. Using rubrics also enables more reliable, consistent, and unbiased scoring.

The rubrics for the Performance Assessment Tasks are analytic task-specific rubrics which are customized to each Unit's task. They establish a number of independent categories to evaluate student performance for each activity. Each rubric uses the same scale to ensure uniformity and reliability of scoring: 4 = excellent, 3 = good, 2 = fair, 1 = poor. The four levels of each rubric incorporate ease of use with sufficient discrimination to judge the range of quality in Performance Assessment Tasks. The same descriptors are used to evaluate the total score. The total score provides a convenient way to quantify your assessment of student work.

You may wish to review the rubric and discuss each criterion with the class before students begin the Performance Assessment Task. This will help students understand the expectations of the task and how they will be assessed on their performance. If possible, show your students two or three examples of exemplary works that were scored as "excellent." This will model the standard of excellence, illustrate a diversity of approaches to a performance task, and encourage creativity.

Portfolio Assessment

A **portfolio** is an alternative assessment based on a carefully chosen sample of a student's work that documents the student's growth and progress over time. Portfolios allow you to assess a student's development, chart the evolution of the student's understanding of a subject, and document the student's accomplishments. Portfolios can help you make instructional decisions, assess curricular goals, and communicate with students and parents. They provide an authentic alternative to traditional assessment that connects reading, writing, and Thinking Skills.

Portfolios allow students to maintain a record of their learning and academic achievement, engage in self-assessment, and reflect on their progress. Portfolios promote a sense of student investment in their learning and ownership of their work. As students seriously contemplate their work, they become increasingly reflective, more skilled at self-evaluation, and more confident in their own judgments of quality. Portfolios can foster a sense of pride and accomplishment. By evaluating a cumulative body of their work, students can identify successful learning, remaining difficulties, and direction for future work.

Consider the following questions when developing a portfolio-based assessment strategy:

- What kind of organization and structure will the portfolio have?
- What forms of student work will go into the portfolio?
- How and when will the student work be selected?
- How will the portfolio be evaluated?

Involve students in these decisions as much as possible. Allowing students to make choices provides motivation and promotes student interest. The specific pieces that students choose to include in their portfolios reflect their personalities and may reveal how they view themselves. Some suggested steps for implementing portfolio-based assessment:

- **Introduce the portfolio** by helping students understand what a portfolio is and how they will build their own portfolios. Review the organization of a portfolio. If possible, show students examples of completed portfolios.
- **Involve students** in the selection of the kinds of work to be included in the portfolio. Help students determine the number of items to be included in the portfolio. Discuss the benefits of choosing quality over quantity. Students should thoughtfully select portfolio entries with guidance from you.
- **Establish student responsibility** by reviewing goals and expectations for the portfolio. Inform students about the kinds of work which are acceptable and appropriate. Establish minimum requirements and encourage students to exceed those requirements. Students should keep their portfolio orderly and date all items and entries.

- **Review and reflect** on the portfolio at regular intervals. Establish a conference time to review works-in-progress and select items for portfolios. Set aside a few minutes at the end of an investigation or the completion of a Chapter for students to look over their work and consider what parts to include in their portfolios.
- **Evaluate** student portfolios on a regular basis, such as after the completion of a Unit or at the end of each grading period. This evaluation can include an evaluation sheet for student self-assessment. Encourage students to participate with you when you assess their work.

Possible Portfolio Items	Possible Selection Criteria
• table of contents • student cover letter • entries from the *Science Journal* • Chapter and Unit tests • Performance Assessments • Graphic Organizers • original models • Explore Activities and Quick Labs • Skill Builder activities • self-evaluation sheets • drawings, photographs, artwork • Problems and Puzzles • videotapes, audiocassettes • experimental data • essays • reports on science topics • scientific research	• significant and important work • best work • difficult or complex work • work where something new was learned • work the student is proud of • work selected by student, teacher, and parent • favorite work • work the student would like to do again in a different way • rough draft, revised draft, and finished work • creative work • representative work • work that demonstrates the student's science skills

Student ____________________ **Date** ____________________

Science Portfolio Evaluation Sheet

Growth Area	Items that Demonstrate Growth	Score
Science Concepts		
Science Process Skills		
Scientific Reasoning Skills		
Investigation Skills		
Scientific Research		
Science Journal Entries		
Cooperative Learning		
Self-Assessment		
4 = exceptional growth (27–32) 3 = substantial growth (21–26) 2 = adequate growth (14–20) 1 = inadequate growth (8–13)	**Total Score**	

Additional Comments: ____________________

Informal Assessment

Informal assessment is the assessment of students through casual observation, informal interviews, anecdotal criteria, and nonstandardized procedures. Informal assessment allows you to measure the day-to-day progress of students and the effectiveness of instruction.

Observation

Observation is an informal assessment of student learning which is based on watching and listening to students as they work. Classroom observation is often used to evaluate student learning when students are working with a partner or a group of students in investigation or performance tasks that require teamwork and cooperation. Observation is an ongoing process that provides insight into the student's attitude, learning style, strengths and weaknesses, and problem-solving techniques. Observations can often capture the spontaneous nature of student creativity and the essence of student performance. They contribute to a more complete picture of student progress.

The following guidelines are recommended when using classroom observation for student assessment:

- Use the same checklist or set of criteria for all students.
- Observe each student several times and at different times of day.
- Observe each student in a variety of situations.
- Evaluate a variety of skills and behaviors for each student.
- Record observations and evaluations as soon as possible.

Interview

An **interview** is an informal assessment of student learning based on conversations with students about their work or on their verbal responses to questions. Student interviews can be conducted individually or with groups of students. They can provide insight into a student's thought processes, attitudes, depth of understanding, and misconceptions. An interview can help you gauge the developmental level of a student and identify Science Process Skills that need reinforcement.

As you listen to and evaluate student responses, ask additional questions to clarify and extend their answers. Interviews can prompt students to reflect on their work and organize their thoughts. Interviews can be used to ascertain student strengths and weaknesses, accommodate student interests and attitudes, identify student learning styles, and modify instructional strategies.

Generic questions that can be asked during a student interview include:

- How could you do this better next time?
- What did you like best about this activity?
- What did you learn by doing this experiment?
- Can you explain this (idea, concept, procedure) in a different way?
- How did you get your answer?
- Is there another way to get the answer?
- What caused that to happen?
- What would happen if you changed this (variable, quantity)?
- Can you think of another example of this (process, thing, event)?

Self-Assessment

Self-assessment is student-generated assessment in which students analyze and evaluate their own performances, strengths and weaknesses, attitudes and interests, and needs for improvement. Self-assessment gives students a chance to review and reflect on their own work. Such reflection also provides students with insight about the direction of any future learning they want to pursue. Self-assessment empowers and motivates students by giving them a feeling of self-control over their work and a sense of responsibility for their own learning. Self-reflection also helps students develop the metacognitive skills they need to learn effectively.

Inexperienced students especially need to practice self-assessment. Initially, students may be too critical of their work. With time and experience, they will become comfortable enough with self-assessment to honestly evaluate their accomplishments and needs for improvement, and their judgments will become more accurate. Some suggestions for implementing self-assessment include:

- Inform students that self-assessment is an exploratory exercise designed to help them find out more about themselves.
- Tell students that there are no right or wrong answers. Their self-assessment responses will not be graded or will receive only a completion grade.
- Encourage students to be honest and objective, not overly critical.
- Model self-assessment for your students by evaluating your own performance.
- Distribute the appropriate self-assessment checklist and rubric (see pages 33 and 34) after students finish an investigation. Before they complete the checklists, review the questions and rubric categories with the students.

Name ____________________ Date ____________________

Student Evaluation: Checklist and Rubric

How did you do? Give yourself the score that best describes your work. Circle the number that tells how you did.	I can do better.	I did well enough	I was good at this.	I was very good at this.
1. I was ready to work.	1	2	3	4
2. I listened to directions.	1	2	3	4
3. I followed instructions.	1	2	3	4
4. I asked questions when I did not understand.	1	2	3	4
5. I used my time wisely.	1	2	3	4
6. I worked well on my own.	1	2	3	4

Answer each question about your work.

7. What did you have trouble with? ____________________

____

8. What was the most important thing you learned? ____________________

____

9. What could you do better at? ____________________

____

10. What were you best at? ____________________

____

11. What part did you enjoy the most? ____________________

____

12. What would you like to learn more about? ____________________

____

Name ____________ Date ____________ Group ____________

Group Evaluation: Checklist and Rubric

How did your group do? Circle the number that best describes how your group worked together.	We can do better.	We did well enough.	We were good at this.	We were very good at at this.
1. We were ready to work.	1	2	3	4
2. We listened to each other's ideas and suggestions.	1	2	3	4
3. We disagreed in a respectful way.	1	2	3	4
4. We solved problems together.	1	2	3	4
5. We helped each other.	1	2	3	4
6. We used our time wisely.	1	2	3	4
7. We shared work and responsibility as a team.	1	2	3	4
8. We completed our task.	1	2	3	4

Answer these questions about your group's work.

9. What was one problem your group had? ____________

____

10. What was your group best at? ____________

____

11. What could your group do better at? ____________

____

12. How did you help your group? ____________

____

Test-Taking Strategies for Students

Prepare: Things to do before you take a test

- Ask your teacher lots of questions! What kind of test will it be? What will be on the test?
- If you do not understand something, ask questions before you take the test. Ask your teacher to explain if you don't understand his or her answers.
- Study your notes, activity sheets, and handouts carefully. Rewrite your notes or put important information on note cards.
- Review material from your Science Book by rereading the assigned pages, writing an outline, or making a graphic organizer.
- Study your Science Words. Make sure you understand what they mean, don't just memorize the definition. Write the meaning of Science Words in your own words.
- Study the models, graphs, charts, and tables from the assigned reading in your Science Book. What do these diagrams show? Make sure you understand the Science Words in the diagrams.
- Make sure you know the answers to the questions at the beginning of each section in your Science Book.
- Pay close attention to the questions in the Topic, Chapter, and Unit Reviews in your Science Book. Some of these questions may be on the test. If you don't know the answers, ask more questions!
- Don't just memorize facts. Learn the ideas of science, the why and the how of science, and the cause and effect of science.
- Get a good night's sleep and eat a good breakfast before you take the test.

Pay Attention: Things to do when you take a test

- Listen to your teacher's directions and read the instructions on the test carefully. If you do not understand something, ask your teacher to explain.
- Look over the test before you begin. Decide which questions are easy and which questions will take the most time. Plan how you will use your time.
- Don't spend too much time on one question, but don't rush. Do the easy questions first, check how much time is left, then plan how you will use the remaining time to answer the more difficult questions.
- Read the test questions carefully and think about what you are reading. Read each question twice before you answer it. Make sure you understand what the question is asking before you answer it.
- If a question asks for a long, written answer, carefully think about how you will answer the question. Organize your thoughts. Plan what you will write before you begin writing.
- If you have enough time, check your answers carefully. Make sure you have completed all of the questions.
- Relax, concentrate, and do the best you can.

Glossary

Alternative Assessment assessment that does not involve a standardized test with traditional assessment items

Authentic Assessment assessment that measures student performance in a real-life task, relevant situation, or purposeful problem that is worthwhile, meaningful, and significant

Closed Question objective assessment item, such as a multiple-choice question, where the correct answer is not open to interpretation

Extended Response Question traditional assessment item that requires the student to provide a written explanation, drawing, or diagram

Graphic Organizer graphic representation of written and verbal statements

Informal Assessment assessment of students through casual observation, informal interviews, anecdotal criteria, and nonstandardized procedures

Interview informal assessment of student learning based on conversations with students about their work or on their verbal responses to questions

Journal alternative assessment based on a written record of a student's thoughts about the subject matter he or she is studying

Observation informal assessment of student learning based on watching and listening to students as they work

Performance Assessment alternative assessment involving an open-ended task or a hands-on activity which is designed to measure student performance against a specific set of criteria

Portfolio alternative assessment based on a carefully chosen sample of a student's work that documents the student's growth and progress over time

Rubric set of scoring criteria used to evaluate student work and assess student performance

Science Process Skills skills that students learn as they carry out scientific inquiry. Instead of a single scientific method, students employ a variety of Process Skills when they are actively involved in scientific investigation

Self-Assessment student-generated assessment where a student analyzes and evaluates his or her own performance, strengths and weaknesses, attitudes and interests, and needs for improvement

Traditional Assessment assessment using both conventional extended-response questions and traditional closed questions, such as multiple choice, true or false, fill-in-the-blank, and matching, on a standardized test

References

Airasian, P., *Classroom Assessment*, Second Edition. New York: McGraw-Hill, 1994.

Brandt, R.S., *Readings from Educational Leadership: Performance Assessment.* Alexandria, VA: Association for Supervision and Curriculum Development, 1992.

Capper, J., *Testing to Learn—Learning to Test.* Washington, DC, Academy for Educational Development. Newark, DE: International Reading Association, 1996.

Farr, B.P., and E. Trumbull, *Assessment Alternatives for Diverse Classrooms.* Norwood, MS: Christopher-Gordon Publishers, 1997.

Lowery, L.F., ed., *Pathways to the Science Standards: Elementary School Edition.* Arlington, VA: National Science Teachers Association, 1997.

National Research Council, *National Science Education Standards.* Washington, DC: National Academy Press, 1996.

Raisen, S., et al., *Assessment in Elementary School Science: The Middle Years.* Washington, DC: The National Center for Improving Science Education, 1990.

Grade 3
Raising Math
Test Scores

The Test-Takers' Handbook

Wow! Here it is again, that test-taking time of year. Are you ready? Are you feeling cool? Whether you get really nervous or you see tests as an interesting challenge, you can probably improve your performance with some test-taking strategies.

Look through this handbook for ways to get ready for a test, catch easy mistakes, and avoid traps. You, too, may become a better test-taker than you are now.

Take the Test-Taking Challenge: Hints for Test-Taking Success

Do you think that Michael Jordan goes straight into a big game, or does he go to practice first? As you take quizzes and tests in math and in other subjects, think about the following hints and strategies and practice as many as you can. In no time, tests will just be a slam-dunk challenge for you.

It Takes Practice

When you know that you have a big test coming, set up some practice sessions to get yourself in shape.

1 **Gather information.** Ask your teacher what topics are going to be tested, and what kinds of questions the test will have:

- ★ multiple choice?
- ★ grids?
- ★ short answer?
- ★ long answer?

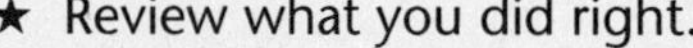

2 **Look back.** Check the work you have already done and that has been corrected. Check old tests and quizzes. Skim lessons that you really understand, and reread lessons you had trouble with.

- ★ Review what you did right.
- ★ Make sure you understand what you did wrong.

3 **Practice.** One good way to practice for a test is to take a practice test. You can even make up your own practice test as a way to study. You can write your answers too.

Relax and show what you know.

It's OK to be a little nervous when test time rolls around — it happens to many of us. Once you get past the first few items, you should be fine.

Whenever you get nervous, remind yourself that you are prepared and you can relax. Then take a deep breath, and then take another one. Say, *"I am ready. I can do this."* Then just do your best.

Review math strategies that you already know. Try strategies such as:

- ★ use estimation
- ★ work backward
- ★ draw a picture
- ★ solve a simpler problem

1+2=3

✔✔ Double Check ✔✔

- ★ When you finish a problem, ask yourself these questions:
  - ☐ Is my answer reasonable?
  - ☐ Does my answer make sense?
  - ☐ Did I answer the question?
  - ☐ Did I include every step?
- ★ Use inverse operations to check your answer.
- ★ Decide if your answer should be greater than or less than the numbers in the problem. Then check if you used the correct operation.

Tick, Tick, Tick

Most tests are timed, but time can be on your side if you play it smart.

- ★ Prepare ahead of time. Tests are usually not a surprise, so take the time to study before they happen.
- ★ Skip items that you are not sure of and come back to them later, but **don't** lose your place on the answer sheet!
- ★ Give more time to items that are worth more. Usually questions that have long answers are worth more than multiple choice.
- ★ Use mental math when you can. It's fast.

Sometimes it helps to close your eyes when you are stuck and visualize similar work you have done before.

Classic Mistakes to Avoid

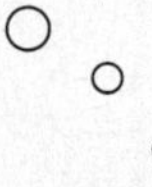

You know better!

Did you know that test writers consider the kinds of mistakes students often make and use them for some answer choices? Use these hints to avoid common errors:

★ Make sure you follow any signs to add, subtract, multiply, or divide.

★ Check your regrouping. Be especially careful with zeros.

★ Line up the digits correctly when you set up computations. For whole numbers, line up on the ones place. For money and decimals, line up the decimal points.

★ Be careful, not careless, about number facts.

★ Subtract the lesser number from the greater number.

Choose Wisely: Taking Multiple-Choice Tests

Multiple-choice questions can be the easiest items on a test. Why? Because you already know that one of the answers given is the right answer. All you have to do is figure out which one it is.

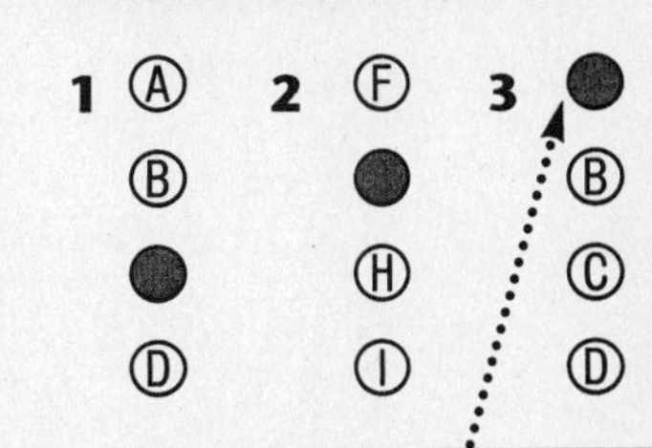

If you are using an answer sheet, make sure that you completely fill in the correct letter for each item. Be careful if you skip items.

Remember to circle only one letter.

❶ Sally and her mother drove 27 miles north from home to a shopping mall. Then they turned and drove 14 miles south to have lunch at a café. How many miles is the café from home?

A 31
B 14
Ⓒ 13
D 12

27
−14
13

If you can't solve the problem mentally, use the white space beside the problem, or a scrap of paper for your work.

Sometimes you can tell that one of the answers doesn't make sense. You can eliminate that choice right away.

❷ A pack of 6 colored markers costs $3.49. If Rob gives $5.00 to buy the markers, how much change will he get back?

F $1.49
Ⓖ $1.51
H $2.29
I $8.49

❸ At the Science Center Gift Shop, Lucy spends $10.95 for a book on dinosaurs and $4.30 for a pencil box. How much did she spend in all?

Ⓐ $15.25
B $15.95
C $14.65
D $14.25

$10.95
+ $4.50
$15.45

If the answer you got is not one of the choices given, go back to the problem.

* Check that you answered the right question.
* Check the numbers you copied.
* Check your calculations.

It's Your Turn: Taking Multiple-Choice Tests

Read each problem below carefully. Then completely fill in the circle for your answer.

Answer Sheet

1	2	3
Ⓐ	Ⓕ	Ⓐ
Ⓑ	Ⓖ	Ⓑ
Ⓒ	Ⓗ	Ⓒ
Ⓓ	Ⓘ	Ⓓ

❶ Which one does **not** name 472?

Read carefully.

A 4 hundreds 7 tens 2 ones
B 47 tens 2 ones
C 47 hundreds 2 ones
D 472 ones

❷ Chloe visits the Children's Museum and then its gift shop. She bought one of these gifts and paid for it with a $20-bill. If her change was a $5-bill and 2 quarters, what did Chloe buy?

$9.95
$14.50
$7.45
$13.99

F paintbrush and paints
G tambourine
H art smock
I maracas

❸ Several classes collected aluminum cans for a recycling drive. What is the range of cans collected?

Class A	85
Class B	36
Class C	67
Class D	175

A 36
B 139
C 175
D 211

Estimate to check the reasonableness of your answers.

✔ Are You Sure? ✔

Before turning in a test, go back one last time to check.

☐ I understood and answered the questions asked.
☐ I checked all my calculations.
☐ My answers make sense.

ANSWERS: See page 97.

Line It Up: Using Answer Grids

For some tests that you will take, you will have to put your answers in grids like the ones below. Don't get nervous! Grids are as easy as 1 - 2 - 3!

It's not that hard. Let's look at some examples.

Answer Grids

1. Solve the problem just as you normally do.
2. Write your answer in the box at the top of the grid.
3. Carefully fill in the matching digits directly below the number you wrote.

❶ Jody's Books sold 728 books last month. Of the books sold 325 of them were fiction and 173 were poetry. The rest of the sales were non-fiction books. How many non-fiction books were sold? Write your answer in the grid.

Write your answer in the box. Start on the left or right, but don't leave *any* blank spaces between parts of your answer.

	2	3	0
⓪	⓪	⓪	●
①	①	①	①
②	●	②	②
③	③	●	③
④	④	④	④
⑤	⑤	⑤	⑤
⑥	⑥	⑥	⑥
⑦	⑦	⑦	⑦
⑧	⑧	⑧	⑧
⑨	⑨	⑨	⑨

Work Space

$$\begin{array}{r} 325 \\ +173 \\ \hline 498 \end{array} \qquad \begin{array}{r} \overset{6\ 12}{\cancel{7}\cancel{2}8} \\ -498 \\ \hline 230 \end{array}$$

Use the ***Work Space*** by the grid or scrap paper if you can't solve a problem mentally.

Fill in the circles below each number that you wrote. Don't forget to fill in for any zeros, too!

❷ Marie has the following coins in her piggy bank.

She found a dime on the sidewalk. How much money does she have now? Write your answer in the grid

When the answer has a decimal point, the point will always be printed in the grid. You do not need to fill in any circle for the decimal point.

$	0	.	9	1
⓪	●		⓪	⓪
①	①		①	●
②	②		②	②
③	③		③	③
④	④		④	④
⑤	⑤		⑤	⑤
⑥	⑥		⑥	⑥
⑦	⑦		⑦	⑦
⑧	⑧		⑧	⑧
⑨	⑨		●	⑨

Do not leave blank spaces before or after the decimal point.

It's Your Turn: Practicing Questions with Answer Grids

Read the problem below carefully. One of the grids has been correctly filled in. Find that grid.

❶ Which figure has a greater perimeter?
Write the greater perimeter in the grid.

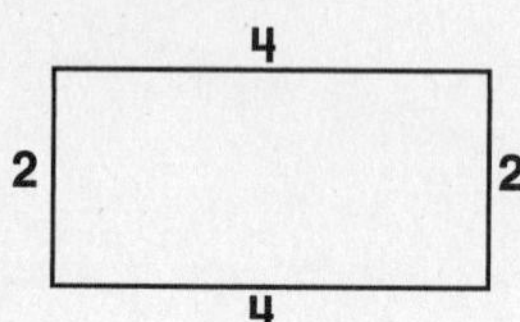

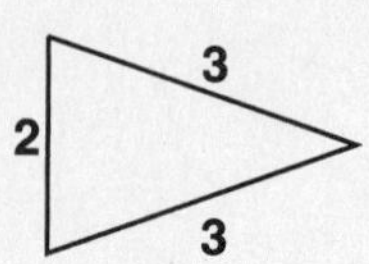

A

	1		2
0	0	0	0
1	●	1	1
2	2	2	●
3	3	3	3
4	4	4	4
5	5	5	5
6	6	6	6
7	7	7	7
8	8	8	8
9	9	9	9

B

1	2		
0	0	0	0
●	●	1	1
2	2	2	2
3	3	3	3
4	4	4	4
5	5	5	5
6	6	6	6
7	7	7	7
8	8	8	8
9	9	9	9

C

		1	2
0	0	0	0
1	1	●	1
2	2	2	●
3	3	3	3
4	4	4	4
5	5	5	5
6	6	6	6
7	7	7	7
8	8	8	8
9	9	9	9

Read the problem below carefully. Then fill in the grid to show your answer.

❷ Gary bought pencils for $1.25 and a pad of paper for $1.89. He gave the clerk a $5 bill. How much change should he get back?

$

		.		
0	0		0	0
1	1		1	1
2	2		2	2
3	3		3	3
4	4		4	4
5	5		5	5
6	6		6	6
7	7		7	7
8	8		8	8
9	9		9	9

ANSWERS: See page 97.

✔ Are You Sure? ✔

Before you turn in your test, check that your grids are carefully filled in.

- ☐ I checked my solution to the problem.
- ☐ I only wrote one digit in each answer box.
- ☐ I checked that the numbers in the box matched my answer. Then I followed down each column and checked that the correct circle was filled in.

Use Your Own Words: Answering Short-Answer Questions

Some problems in a test are just like other math activities you do—you have to write your own answer on a line or in a space shown. Short-answer questions may ask you to:

- ★ solve a problem and show your work.
- ★ explain how you got your answer.
- ★ draw a picture, diagram, graph, or table.
- ★ write a problem.

So, what's the plan?

You can use the steps you use when solving problems to plan your answer.

READ What question do you need to answer?

PLAN What do you need to do?

SOLVE What steps will you take to solve the problem?

LOOK BACK Does your answer make sense?

Mr. Murphy works for a soup company. He is checking the number of cans on some supermarket shelves. He sees that there are two shelves with his soup. Each shelf has three rows of cans with three cans in each row. Draw a picture to show the cans of soup on the shelves. Then show how to find the total number of cans using numbers. Tell why your answer is reasonable.

Work Space

Always show your work. Even if you make a small error, you may get partial credit if you show you understand how to solve the problem.

3 x 3 = 9

3 x 3 = 9

9 + 9 = 18

There are 18 cans of soup. My answer is reasonable because there are three rows of the cans or 9 cans on the first shelf. You can add 9 + 9 or multiply 2 x 9 for the two shelves to get 18 cans.

Make sure you answer the questions.

Explain how you got your answer and tell why your answer is reasonable.

Test-Taking Hint: Short-answer and long-answer questions are usually worth more points than multiple-choice or grid questions. Plan your time.

Put It All Together: Writing Long Answers to Questions

How are long-answer questions different from short-answer questions? You guessed it! It takes longer to answer them, and they usually have more than one step. They are usually worth more points.

Try this long-answer question.

Mark has **all of the same kind** of coins in his pocket. He does not have any pennies. His coins total one dollar. Make a list of all of the possible types of coins Mark could have. Also show how many of each coin he would have.

Work Space

Use your list to make a graph of the number of each type of coin you need to equal one-dollar.

Be sure to:

- write a title for the graph.
- list each type of coin below the graph.
- carefully graph the data.

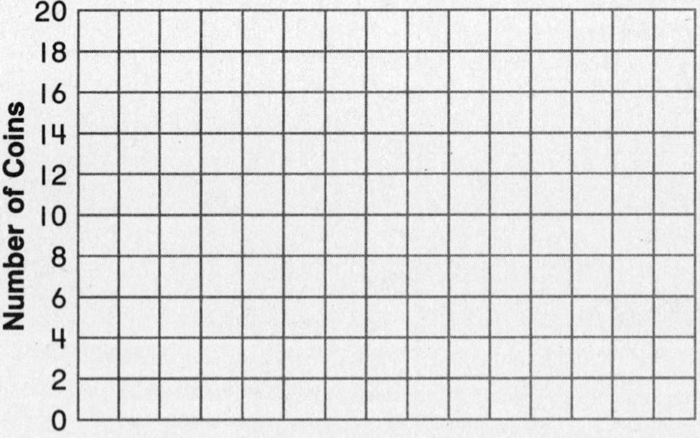

Mathematics Reference Sheet

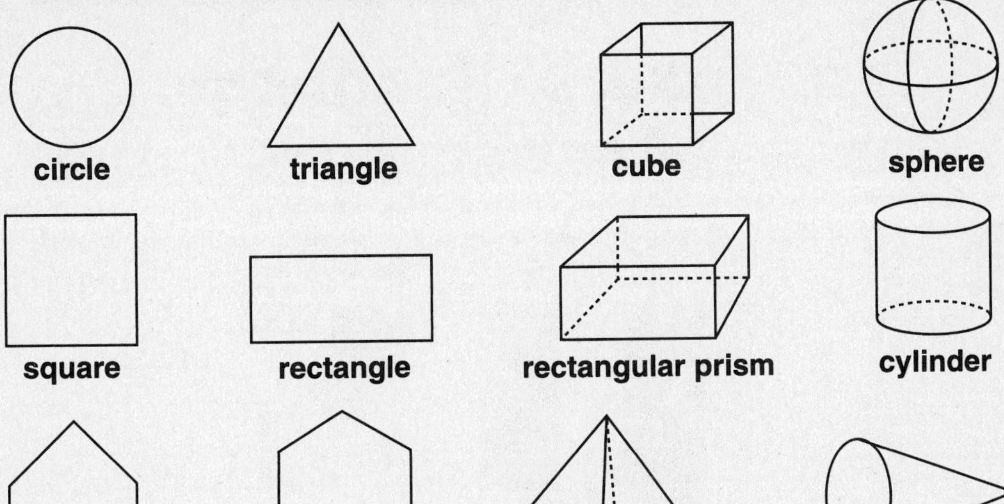

Measurement

Customary

Length
I foot (ft) = 12 inches (in.)
I yard (yd) = 3 feet
I yard = 36 inches

Capacity
I pint (pt) = 2 cups
I quart (qt) = 2 pints
I gallon (gal) = 4 quarts

Weight
I pound (lb) = 16 ounces (oz)

Temperature

degrees Fahrenheit (°F)
water freezes: 32°F
water boils: 212°F

Metric Units

Length
I meter = 100 centimeters (cm)
I meter = 10 decimeters (dm)
I decimeter = 10 centimeters

Capacity
1,000 milliliters (mL) = I liter (L)

Mass
I kilogram (kg) = 1,000 grams (g)

degrees Celsius (°C)
water freezes: 0°C
water boils: 100°C

Time
I minute (min) = 60 seconds
I hour (h) = 60 minutes
I day (d) = 24 hours
I year (yr) = 12 months (mo)
I year = 365 days

Perimeter and Area
Perimeter = 3 + 4 + 3 + 4 = 14 units
Area = 12 square units

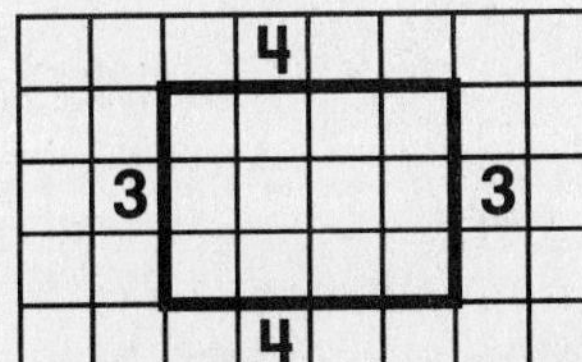

Test-Takers' Handbook: Answers

Here are answers to the test questions you tried so far.

Page 44: ❶ C, ❷ G, ❸ A

Page 46: ❶ Grid C ❷

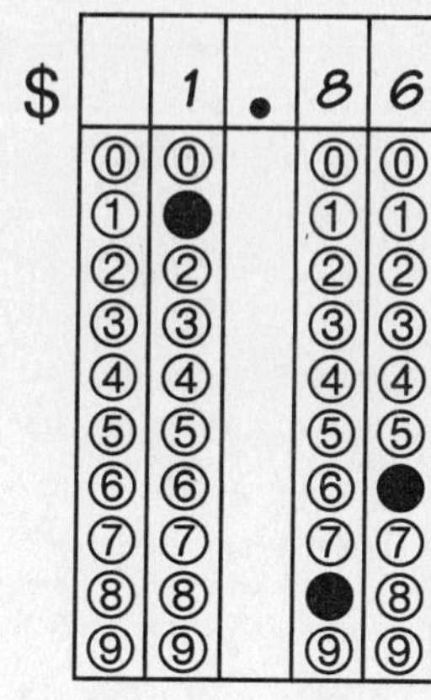

Page 48: Answers may vary. A possible list of the types of coins he might have is:
Quarters
Dimes
Nickels

He might have 4 quarters, 10 dimes, 20 nickels. The graph might look like this.

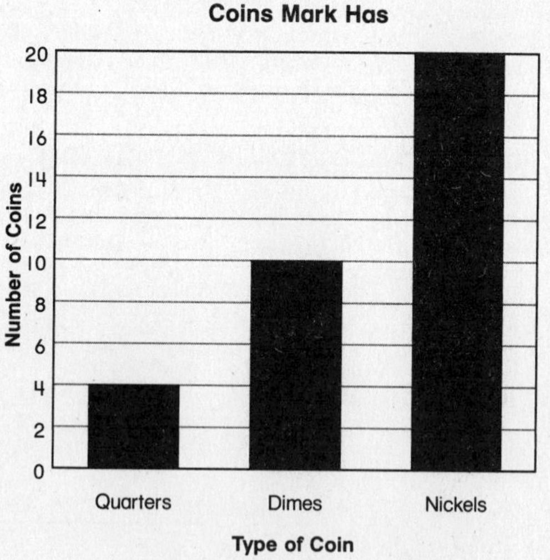

McGraw-Hill School Division

Grade 4
Raising Math Test Scores

The Test-Takers' Handbook

Wow! Here it is again, that test-taking time of year. Are you ready? Are you feeling cool? Are you scared? No matter how you feel about tests, you can probably improve your performance with some test-taking strategies.

Look through this handbook for ways to get ready for a test, catch easy mistakes, and avoid traps. You, too, may become a better test-taker!

Take the Test-Taking Challenge: Hints for Test-Taking Success

Do you think that Michael Jordan goes straight into a big game, or does he go to practice first? As you take quizzes and tests in math and in other subjects, think about the following hints and strategies, and practice as many as you can. In no time, tests will just be a slam-dunk challenge for you.

It Takes Practice

When you know that you have a big test coming, set up some practice sessions to get yourself in shape.

1 **Gather information.** Ask your teacher what topics are going to be tested, and what kinds of questions the test will have:

★ multiple choice?

Sue read from 3:30 to 4:15.
For how many minutes did she read?
A 45
B 60
C 75
D 90

★ open answer?

1 Jon wants to buy a pen that costs $1.75.
A. He has 6 quarters, 3 dimes,1 nickel, and 5 pennies. How much money does he have?
$1.80
B. Does he have enough money to buy the pen? Explain how you found out.
He has $1.80. $1.80 > $1.75, so he can buy the pen.

2 **Look back.** Check the work you have already done and that has been corrected. Check old tests and quizzes. Skim lessons that you really understand, and reread lessons you had trouble with.

★ Review what you did right.
★ Make sure you understand what you did wrong.

3 **Practice.** One good way to practice for a test is to take a practice test. You can even make up your own practice test as a way to study. You can write your answers too!

Relax and show what you know.

It's OK to be a little nervous when test time rolls around—it happens to many of us. Once you get past the first few items, you should be fine.

Whenever you get nervous, remind yourself that you are prepared and you can relax. Then take a deep breath, and then take another one. Say, *"I am ready. I can do this."* Then just do your best.

Review math strategies that you already know. Try strategies such as:

★ use estimation

★ work backward

★ draw a picture

★ solve a simpler problem

1+2=3

✔✔ DoubleCheck ✔✔

- When you finish a problem, ask yourself these questions:
  - ★ Is my answer reasonable?
  - ★ Does my answer make sense?
  - ★ Did I answer the question?
  - ★ Did I include every step?
- Use inverse operations to check your answer. For example, if you add to find an answer, then subtract to check.
- Decide if your answer should be greater than or less than the numbers in the problem. Then check if you used the correct operation.

Tick, Tick, Tick

Most tests are timed, but time can be on your side if you play it smart.

★ Prepare ahead of time. Tests are usually not a surprise, so take the time to study before they happen.

★ Skip items that you are not sure of and come back to them later, but **don't** lose your place on the answer sheet!

★ Give more time to items that are worth more. Usually, questions that have open answers are worth more than multiple choice.

★ Use mental math when you can. It's faster than paper and pencil.

Sometimes it helps to close your eyes when you are stuck and visualize similar work you have done before.

Classic Mistakes to Avoid

I wrote the answer in the wrong place. Now I'm all mixed up.

I didn't see that in the directions!

This answer doesn't make sense, but it's one of the choices, so it must be right.

These choices are wrong. They don't match my answer.

You know better!

Did you know that test writers consider the kinds of mistakes students often make and use them for some answer choices? Use these hints to avoid common errors:

★ Make sure you follow any signs to add, subtract, multiply, or divide.

★ Check your regrouping. Be especially careful with zeros.

★ Line up the digits correctly when you add, subtract, multiply, or divide. For whole numbers, line up digits on the ones place.

★ Be careful, not careless, about number facts.

★ Subtract the lesser number from the greater number.

★ When dividing, consider your remainder.

Choose Wisely: Taking Multiple-Choice Tests

Multiple-choice questions can be the easiest items on a test. Why? Because you already know that one of those answers given is the right answer. All you have to do is figure out which one it is.

Answer Sheet

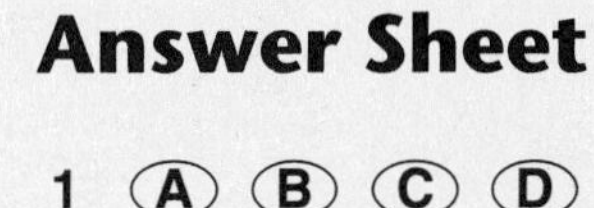

Remember to fill in only one circle on your answer sheet.

1 **Kate estimates the difference between \$4.84 and \$1.24 by rounding to the nearest ten cents. Which of the following shows her estimate?**

A \$5.00 − \$1.00 = \$4.00
B \$4.80 − \$1.00 = \$3.80
C \$4.80 − \$1.20 = \$3.60
D \$4.80 − \$1.30 = \$3.50

\$4.84 rounds to \$4.80
\$1.24 rounds to \$1.20

$$\begin{array}{r} \$4.80 \\ -\ 1.20 \\ \hline \$3.60 \end{array}$$

If you can't solve the problem mentally, use the white space beside the problem, or a scrap of paper for your work.

2 **Juan is thinking of the greatest number that, when rounded to the nearest hundred, rounds to five thousand. What number is he thinking of?**

A 4,999
B 5,049
C 5,099
D 6,099

Sometimes you can tell that one of the answers doesn't make sense. You can eliminate that choice right away.

Some multiple-choice questions present information in the problem, in graphs, tables, charts, or in a picture. You need to interpret the information to solve the problem.

SALE

TUNA FISH	$1.37 per can
WHITE BREAD	$0.99 per loaf
MAYONNAISE	$1.79 per can

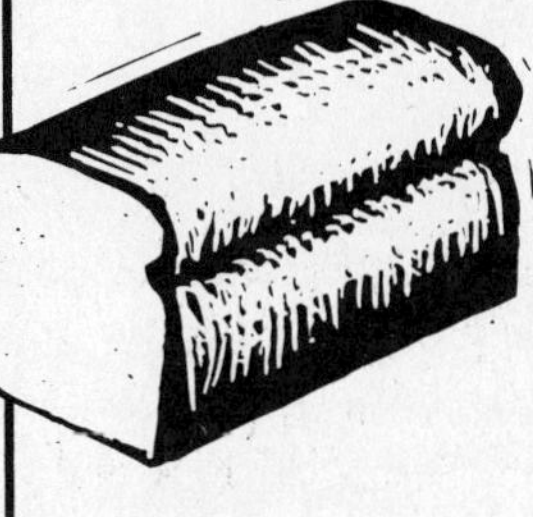

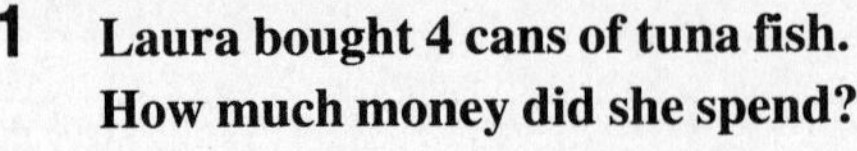

1 **Laura bought 4 cans of tuna fish. How much money did she spend?**

A $1.39
B $3.96
Ⓒ $5.48
D $7.16

$1.37
x 4
$5.48

If the answer you got is not one of the choices given, go back to the problem.

★ Check the numbers you copied.
★ Check that you performed the correct operation.
★ Check your calculations.

If you are using an answer sheet, make sure that you completely fill in the correct letter for each item. Be careful if you skip items.

Answer Sheet

1 Ⓐ Ⓑ Ⓒ Ⓓ
2 Ⓐ Ⓑ Ⓒ Ⓓ

It's Your Turn: Practicing Multiple-Choice Questions

Try these multiple-choice questions.

Answer Sheet

1 (A) (B) (C) (D)

2 (A) (B) (C) (D)

3 (A) (B) (C) (D)

Read each question carefully. Then completely fill in the correct circle on the answer sheet.

1 **How do you write six thousand, fifty in standard form?**

A 650
B 6,005
C 6,050
D 6,500

Read carefully.

2 **In the table below, what does the number 2 stand for in tl number that tells how long the Baton Rouge bridge is?**

BRIDGES IN THE UNITED STATES		
NAME	**LOCATION**	**LENGTH OF MAIN SPAN (in feet)**
Greater New Orleans	Mississippi River, New Orleans, LA	1,575
Brooklyn	East River, Manhattan–Brooklyn, NY	1,596
Baton Rouge	Mississippi River, Baton Rouge, LA	1,235
Golden Gate	Golden Gate Strait, San Francisco, CA	4,200

A 2,000
B 200
C 20
D 2

Check that you used the correct data from the table.

3 **Which one of the following number sentences is correct?**

A $629 - 255 = 255 - 629$
B $15 + 167 = 167 - 15$
C $(12 + 52) + 39 = (12 + 52) + (12 + 39)$
D $73 + 568 = 568 + 73$

✔ Are You Sure? ✔

Before turning in a test, go back one last time to check.

☐ I understood and answered the questions asked.

☐ I checked my calculations for errors.

☐ My answers make sense.

Use Your Own Words: Answering Open-Answer Questions

How are open-answer questions different from multiple-choice questions? You guessed it! There are no answer choices given – the answer is open for *you* to complete. Usually open-answer questions take longer to answer than multiple choice, and they may have more than one step. They are usually worth more points.

Open-answer questions are just like other math activities you do–you have to write your own answer on a line or in a space shown. These questions may ask you to:

★ solve a problem and show your work.
★ explain how you got your answer.
★ draw a picture, diagram, graph, or table.
★ write a problem.

The Sneaker Store is having a close-out sale on sneakers. They have pairs of sneakers in only 3 sizes left. They are available in red, white, and black. If they have 25 pairs of each kind of sneaker, how can you determine how many pairs of sneakers are on sale?

Work Space

$3 \times 3 = 9$

$25 \times 9 = 225$

They have 3 sizes in 3 colors, so the total number of choices is 9. You need to multiply the number of pairs times each choice.

The Sneaker Store has 225 pairs of sneakers on sale.

Always show your work. Even if you make a small error, you may get partial credit if you show you understand how to solve the problem.

Explain how you got your answer. Tell why your answer is reasonable.

Make sure you answer the question!

It's Your Turn: Practicing Open-Answer Questions

Try these open-answer questions.

Be sure to:

★ Read the problem carefully.
★ Show your work.
★ Solve the problem, making sure you answer the question.
★ If asked, explain how you got your answer and tell why your answer is reasonable.

So, what's the plan?

You can use the same steps you use when solving problems to plan your answer.

READ What question do you need to answer?

PLAN How will you answer the question?

SOLVE What exactly will you do? In what order?

LOOK BACK How can you check that your answer makes sense?

You want to buy a book that costs $3.50. You empty out your piggy bank and find out that you have the amount of money shown below.

A **You know that you can trade 10 pennies for 1 dime. Name 3 other trades you can make with the coins above.**

____

____

____

Think of a way to organize this information to make it easier to answer the question.

McGraw-Hill School Division

B Complete each table.

Nickels

Number	1	2	3	4	5	6	7	8	9
Value	5¢								

Dimes

Number	1	2	3	4	5	6	7	8	9
Value	10¢								

C Write >, <, or = to complete this sentence about the value of the coins above.

4 dimes ______ 8 nickels

D Do you have enough money to buy the book you want? Explain how you found out.

____

____

____

____

____

____

____

____

What are you asked to decide?

Remember to include your explanation.

McGraw-Hill School Division

Test-Takers' Handbook: Answers

Here are answers to the test questions you tried so far.

Page 59: **1** C; **2** B; **3** D

Page 61: **A** Answers may vary. Sample given. 2 quarters for 5 dimes; 2 nickels for 1 dime; 5 pennies for 1 nickel)

Page 62: **B** **Nickels**

Number	1	2	3	4	5	6	7	8	9
Value	5¢	10¢	15¢	20¢	25¢	30¢	35¢	40¢	45¢

Dimes

Number	1	2	3	4	5	6	7	8	9
Value	10¢	20¢	30¢	40¢	50¢	60¢	70¢	80¢	90¢

C 4 dimes = 8 nickels

D The piggy bank contained $2.50 in coins. The amount in the piggy bank is less than the cost of the book. You cannot buy the book.

Grade 5
Raising Math Test Scores

The Test-Takers' Handbook

Wow! Here it is again, that test-taking time of year. Are you ready? Are you feeling cool? Whether you get really nervous or you see tests as an interesting challenge, you can probably improve your performance with some test-taking strategies.

Look through this handbook for ways to get ready for a test, catch easy mistakes, and avoid traps. You, too, may become a better test-taker than you are now.

Take the Test-Taking Challenge: Hints for Test-Taking Success

Do you think that Michael Jordan goes straight into a big game, or does he go to practice first? As you take quizzes and tests in math and in other subjects, think about the following hints and strategies and practice as many as you can. In no time, tests will just be a slam-dunk challenge for you.

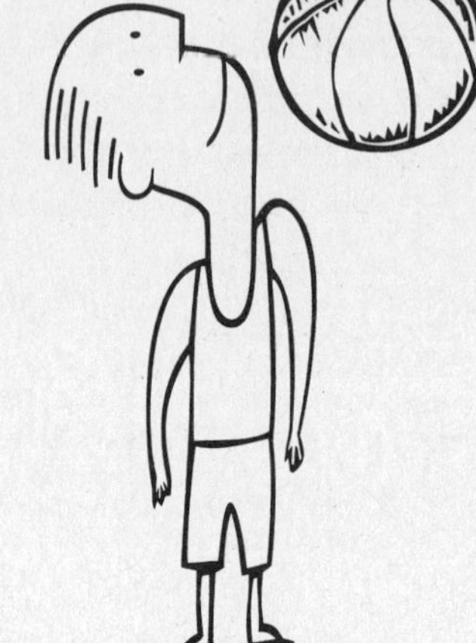

It Takes Practice

When you know that you have a big test coming, set up some practice sessions to get yourself in shape.

1 **Gather information.** Ask your teacher what topics are going to be tested, and what kinds of questions the test will have:

- ★ multiple choice?
- ★ grids?
- ★ short answer?
- ★ long answer?

2 **Look back.** Check the work you have already done and that has been corrected. Check old tests and quizzes. Skim lessons that you really understand, and reread lessons you had trouble with.

- ★ Review what you did right.
- ★ Make sure you understand what you did wrong.

3 **Practice.** One good way to practice for a test is to take a practice test. You can even make up your own practice test as a way to study. You can write your answers too!

Relax and show what you know.

It's OK to be a little nervous when test time rolls around — it happens to many of us. Once you get past the first few items, you should be fine.

Whenever you get nervous, remind yourself that you are prepared and you can relax. Then take a deep breath, and then take another one. Say, *"I am ready. I can do this."* Then just do your best.

Review math strategies that you already know. Try strategies such as:

- ★ use estimation
- ★ work backward
- ★ draw a picture
- ★ solve a simpler problem

1+2=3

✓✓ Double Check ✓✓

★ When you finish a problem, ask yourself these questions:

- ☐ Is my answer reasonable?
- ☐ Does my answer make sense?
- ☐ Did I answer the question?
- ☐ Did I include every step?

★ Use inverse operations to check your answer.

★ Decide if your answer should be greater than or less than the numbers in the problem. Then check if you used the correct operation.

Tick, Tick, Tick

Most tests are timed, but time can be on your side if you play it smart.

- ★ Prepare ahead of time. Tests are usually not a surprise, so take the time to study before they happen.
- ★ Skip items that you are not sure of and come back to them later, but **don't** lose your place on the answer sheet!
- ★ Give more time to items that are worth more. Usually questions that have long answers are worth more than multiple choice.
- ★ Use mental math when you can. It's fast.

Sometimes it helps to close your eyes when you are stuck and visualize similar work you have done before.

Classic Mistakes to Avoid

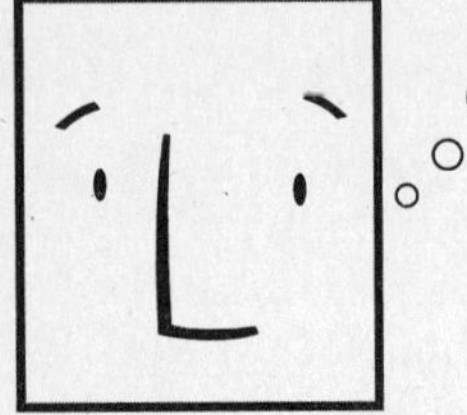

I wrote the answer in the wrong place. Now all my answers mixed up!

I didn't see that in the directons!

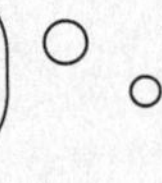

These choices are wrong. They don't match my answer.

This answer doesn't make sense, but it's one of the choices so it must be right.

You know better!

Did you know that test writers consider the kinds of mistakes students often make and use them for some answer choices? Use these hints to avoid common errors:

- ★ Make sure you follow any signs to add, subtract, multiply, or divide.
- ★ Check your regrouping. Be especially careful with zeros.
- ★ Line up the digits correctly when you set up computations. For whole numbers, line up on the ones place. For decimals, line up the decimal points.
- ★ Be careful, not careless, about number facts.
- ★ Subtract the lesser number from the greater number.
- ★ Consider your remainder when dividing.
- ★ Remember to use common denominators when adding and subtracting fractions.

Choose Wisely: Taking Multiple-Choice Tests

Multiple-choice questions can be the easiest items on a test. Why? Because you already know that one of those answers given is the right answer. All you have to do is figure out which one it is.

Answer Sheet

1	2	3
Ⓐ	●	Ⓐ
Ⓑ	Ⓖ	●
●	Ⓗ	Ⓒ
Ⓓ	Ⓘ	Ⓓ

If you are using an answer sheet, make sure that you completely fill in the correct letter for each item. Be careful if you skip items.

Remember to circle only one letter.

❶ Erik has 51 large beads and thousands of small beads. He wants to make necklaces to sell at a local craft fair. He wants to use 3 large beads and 25 small beads to make each necklace. How many necklaces can he make?

A 54
B 48
Ⓒ 17
D 79

$$\begin{array}{r} 17 \\ 3\overline{)51} \\ -3 \\ \hline 21 \\ -21 \\ \hline 0 \end{array}$$

If you can't solve the problem mentally, use the white space beside the problem, or a scrap of paper for your work.

❷ Lauren bought fabric to make a suit. The 4 yards of fabric that she bought cost $68.40. How much does 1 yard of fabric cost?

Ⓕ $17.10
G $12.10
H $18.10
J $273.60

Sometimes you can tell that one of the answers doesn't make sense. You can eliminate that choice right away.

❸ Sarah's team earned 316 more points in the school fitness games than Jon's team did. John's team earned 12 points more than Ashley's team, which earned 135 points. How many points did Sarah's team earn?

A 316
Ⓑ 463
C 304
D 328

$$\begin{array}{r} 135 \\ +\ 12 \\ \hline 147 \end{array}$$

If the answer you got is not one of the choices given, go back to the problem.

* Check that you answered the right question.
* Check the numbers you copied.
* Check your calculations.

It's Your Turn: Taking Multiple-Choice Tests

Read each problem below carefully. Then completely fill in the circle for your answer.

Answer Sheet

1 Ⓐ Ⓑ Ⓒ Ⓓ

2 Ⓕ Ⓖ Ⓗ Ⓘ

3 Ⓐ Ⓑ Ⓒ Ⓓ

1. Which number below shows three hundred sixteen thousand?

   A 30,016,000
   B 316,000
   C 300,160
   D 300,016

Read carefully.

2. This table shows the number of perfect scores on math quizzes for a group of students. Find the mean number of perfect scores for the group.

Student	Perfect Scores
Erik	7
Lauren	8
Sam	5
Dave	10
Gerry	10

Check your calculations.

   F 5
   G 8
   H 10
   I 40

3. Joel cuts three lawns each week for $15 per lawn. He spends $10 each week and saves the rest. How much will Joel have saved in 6 weeks?

   A $30
   B $60
   C $180
   D $210

Estimate to check the reasonableness of your answers.

✔ Check, please ✔

Before turning in a test, go back one last time to check.

- ☐ I understood and answered the questions asked.
- ☐ I checked all my calculations.
- ☐ My answers make sense.

ANSWERS: See page 97.

Line It Up: Using Answer Grids

For some tests that you will take, you will have to put your answers in grids like the ones below. Don't get nervous! Grids are as easy as 1 - 2 - 3 !

Answer Grids

1 Solve the problem just as you normally do.
2 Write your answer in the box at the top of the grid.
3 Carefully fill in the matching digits directly below the number you wrote.

Write your answer in the box. Start on the left or right, but don't leave *any* blank spaces between parts of your answer.

1 In a pattern of numbers, the next number in a sequence is found by multiplying the previous number by 2 and then adding 1.

1, 3, 7, ___, ___, ___, …

What is the seventh number in the sequence? Write your answer in the grid.

	1	2	7
⓪	⓪	⓪	⓪
①	●	①	①
②	②	●	②
③	③	③	③
④	④	④	④
⑤	⑤	⑤	⑤
⑥	⑥	⑥	⑥
⑦	⑦	⑦	●
⑧	⑧	⑧	⑧
⑨	⑨	⑨	⑨

Work Space

Input	1	1	3	4	5	6	7
Output	1	3	7	15	31	63	127

Fill in the circles below each number that you wrote. Don't forget to fill in for any zeros, too!

Use the ***Work Space*** by the grid or scrap paper if you can't solve a problem mentally.

2 Which is less: one and five hundredths or one and five thousandths? Write your answer in standard form in the grid.

When the answer has a decimal point, the point will always be printed in the grid. You do not need to fill in any circle for the decimal point.

	1	.	0	0	5
⓪	⓪		●	●	⓪
①	●		①	①	①
②	②		②	②	②
③	③		③	③	③
④	④		④	④	④
⑤	⑤		⑤	⑤	●
⑥	⑥		⑥	⑥	⑥
⑦	⑦		⑦	⑦	⑦
⑧	⑧		⑧	⑧	⑧
⑨	⑨		⑨	⑨	⑨

Do not leave blank spaces before or after the decimal point.

1.05
1.005
1.0005 < 1.05

It's Your Turn: Practicing Questions with Answer Grids

Read the problem below carefully. One of the grids has been correctly filled in. Find that grid.

1 You entered 2.45 × 5.2 on your calculator and the display showed 127.4. You estimate that the answer should be about 10, so you know that 127.4 is not reasonable. Find the correct product for 2.45 × 5.2.

A

	1	.	2	7
0	0		0	0
1	●		1	1
2	2		●	2
3	3		3	3
4	4		4	4
5	5		5	5
6	6		6	6
7	7		7	●
8	8		8	8
9	9		9	9

B

1	2	.	7	4
0	0		0	0
●	1		1	1
2	●		2	2
3	3		3	3
4	4		4	●
5	5		5	5
6	6		6	6
7	7		●	7
8	8		8	8
9	9		9	9

C

1	2	.	7	4
●	0		0	0
1	1		1	1
2	●		2	2
3	3		3	3
4	4		●	4
5	5		5	5
6	6		6	6
7	7		7	●
8	8		8	8
9	9		9	9

Read the problem below carefully. Then fill in the grid to show your answer.

2 Lisa finds that the exchange rate for U.S. dollars and German marks is one U.S. dollar for every 0.57 marks. How many marks will Lisa get for the $85 spending money that she planned for her trip to Germany?

$			.		
	0	0		0	0
	1	1		1	1
	2	2		2	2
	3	3		3	3
	4	4		4	4
	5	5		5	5
	6	6		6	6
	7	7		7	7
	8	8		8	8
	9	9		9	9

ANSWERS: See page 97.

✓ Are You Sure? ✓

One last time, check that your grids are carefully filled in.

- ☐ I checked my solution to problem.
- ☐ I only wrote one digit in each answer box.
- ☐ I checked that the numbers in box matched my answer. Then I followed down each column and checked that the correct circle was filled in.

Use Your Own Words: Answering Short-Answer Questions

Some problems in a test are just like other math activities you do—you have to write your own answer on a line or in a space shown. Short-answer questions may ask you to:

★ solve a problem and show your work.
★ explain how you got your answer.
★ draw a picture, diagram, graph, or table.
★ write a problem.

So, what's the plan?

You can use the steps you already know to help you solve any math problem.

READ What question do you need to answer?

PLAN What do you need to do?

SOLVE What steps will you take to solve the problem?

LOOK BACK Does your answer make sense?

Always show your work. Even if you make a small error, you may get partial credit if you show you understand how to solve the problem.

You just bought a rack to store your videotapes in. The rack has 3 sections. Each section holds 9 videos. Does the rack have enough space for your 29 videos? Draw a diagram and explain why your answer is reasonable.

Work Space

3 X 9 = 27
27 < 29
29 – 27 = 2

No, there is not enough room for my 29 videos. Multiplying 3 times 9 means that there is only room for 27 videos, and 27 is less than 29. Two of the videos won't fit.

Make sure you answer the question.

Explain how you got your answer and tell why your answer is reasonable.

Test-Taking Hint: Short-answer and long-answer questions are usually worth more points than multiple-choice or grid questions. Plan your time.

Put It All Together: Writing Long Answers to Questions

How are long-answer questions different from short-answer questions? You guessed it! It takes longer to answer them, and they usually have more than one step. They are also usually worth more points.

Try this long-answer question.

The table shows the distances in miles the Hiking Club at Rockville School walked each Saturday during the spring.

Apr. 5	Apr. 12	Apr. 19	Apr. 26	May 3	May 10	May 17	May 24	May 31	June 7
1.5	2.2	0.8	1.6	2.5	1.8	2.5	1.4	3.2	2.5

Write a paragraph for the Rockville School paper describing the activities of the Hiking Club. Include an appropriate graph of the data. In your description include the range, mode, and median and/or mean.

Work Space

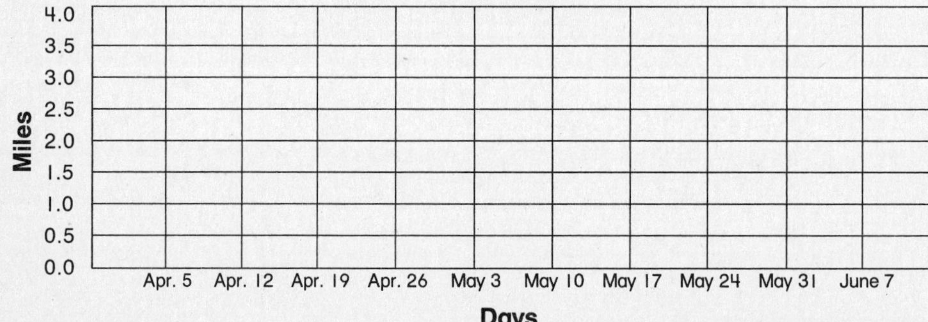

ANSWERS: See page 97.

Test-Takers' Handbook: Answers

Here are answers to the test questions you tried so far.

Page 72: ❶ B, ❷ G, ❸ D

Page 74: ❶ Grid B ❷

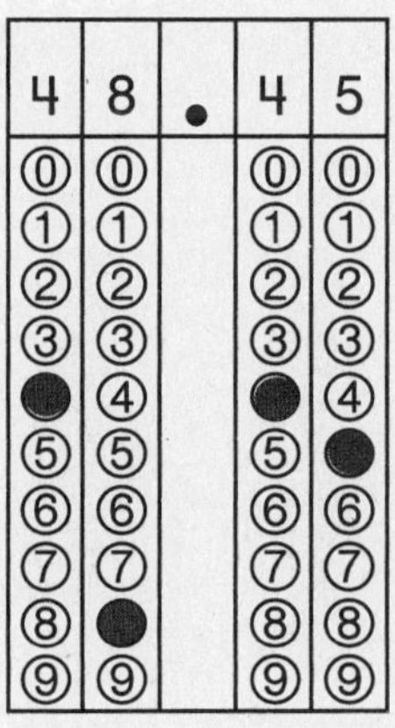

Page 76:

Hiking Club Distances Hiked

Miles: 0.0, 0.5, 1.0, 1.5, 2.0, 2.5, 3.0, 3.5, 4.0

Days: Apr. 5, Apr. 12, Apr. 19, Apr. 26, May 3, May 10, May 17, May 24, May 31, June 7

Student paragraphs will vary. Paragraphs should relate data accurately from the graph and table and should include information about the range, mode, median and/or mean.

Range = 2.4 miles
Mode = 2.5 miles
Median = 2 miles
Mean = 2 miles

Grade 6
Raising Math Test Scores

The Test-Takers' Handbook

Wow! Here it is again, that test-taking time of year. Are you ready? Are you feeling cool? Whether you get really nervous or you see tests as an interesting challenge, you can probably improve your performance with some test-taking strategies.

Look through this handbook for ways to get ready for a test, catch easy mistakes, and avoid traps. You, too, may become a better test-taker than you are now!

Take the Test-Taking Challenge: Hints for Test-Taking Success

Do you think that Michael Jordan goes straight into a big game, or does he go to practice first? As you take quizzes and tests in math and in other subjects, think about the following hints and strategies, and practice as many as you can. In no time, tests will just be a slam-dunk challenge for you.

It Takes Practice

When you know that you have a big test coming, set up some practice sessions to get yourself in shape.

1 **Gather information.** Ask your teacher what topics are going to be tested, and what kinds of questions the test will have:

★ multiple choice?

1 Which set of numbers completes the table below?

Rule: 27 people per plane				
Planes	1	2	3	4
People				

A 27, 28, 29, 30
B 27, 54, 81, 108
C 27, 44, 71, 118
D 28, 29, 30, 31

★ open answer?

2 **Sixteen-ounce packages of Al Dente Pasta cost $1.99 each. How much would 5 packages of the pasta cost? Write your answer on the line below. Show your work.**

____

2 **Look back.** Check the work you have already done and that has been corrected. Check old tests and quizzes. Skim lessons that you really understand, and reread lessons you had trouble with.

★ Review what you did right.
★ Make sure you understand what you did wrong.

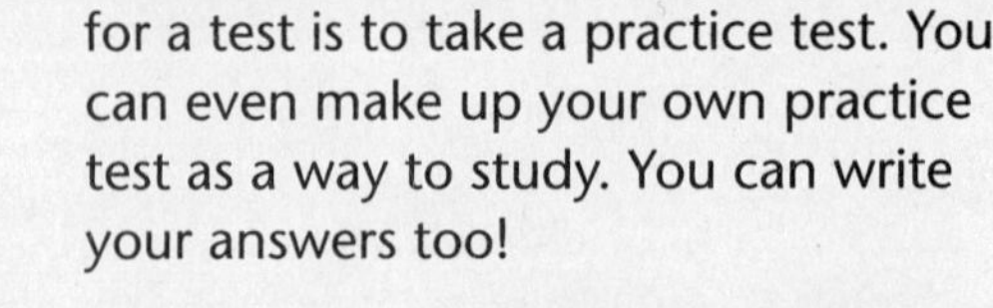

3 **Practice.** One good way to practice for a test is to take a practice test. You can even make up your own practice test as a way to study. You can write your answers too!

Relax and show what you know.

It's OK to be a little nervous when test time rolls around—it happens to many of us. Once you get past the first few items, you should be fine.

Whenever you get nervous, remind yourself that you are prepared and you can relax. Then take a deep breath, and then take another one. Say, *"I am ready. I can do this."* Then just do your best.

Review math strategies that you already know. Try strategies such as:

★ use estimation

★ work backward

★ draw a picture

★ solve a simpler problem

1+2=3

✔✔ Double Check ✔✔

- When you finish a problem, ask yourself these questions:
  - ★ Is my answer reasonable?
  - ★ Does my answer make sense?
  - ★ Did I answer the question?
  - ★ Did I include every step?
- Use inverse operations to check your answer.
- Decide if your answer should be greater than or less than the numbers in the problem. Then check if you used the correct operation.

Tick, Tick, Tick

Most tests are timed, but time can be on your side if you play it smart.

★ Prepare ahead of time. Tests are usually not a surprise, so take the time to study before they happen.

★ Skip items that you are not sure of and come back to them later, but **don't** lose your place on the answer sheet!

★ Give more time to items that are worth more. Usually, questions that have open answers are worth more than multiple choice.

★ Use mental math when you can. It's faster than paper and pencil.

Sometimes it helps to close your eyes when you are stuck and visualize similar work you have done before.

Classic Mistakes to Avoid

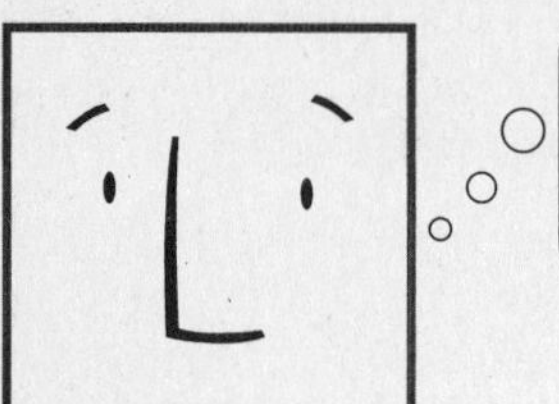

You know better!

Did you know that test writers consider the kinds of mistakes students often make and use them for some answer choices? Use these hints to help you avoid common errors:

- ★ Make sure you follow any signs to add, subtract, multiply, or divide.
- ★ Check your regrouping. Be especially careful with zeros.
- ★ Line up the digits correctly when you add, subtract, multiply, or divide. For whole numbers, line up digits on the ones place. For decimals, line up the decimal points.
- ★ Be careful, not careless, about number facts.
- ★ Consider your remainder when dividing.

Choose Wisely: Taking Multiple-Choice Tests

Multiple-choice questions can be the easiest items on a test. Why? Because you already know that one of those answers given is the right answer. All you have to do is figure out which one it is.

Answer Sheet

1	2	3
(A)	(J)	(A)
(B) ●	(K)	(B)
(C)	(L) ●	(C) ●
(D)	(M)	(D)

If you can't solve the problem mentally, use the white space beside the problem, or a scrap of paper.

1 **The range of Hannah's last five test scores in math is 7. Her two highest scores are 95 and 96. The mode is her lowest grade. The median is 2 points higher than the mode. What is the median of Hannah's test scores?**

A 88
B 89
C 91
D 92

highest
96 95 91 88 89
median mode
96 − 7 = 89

2 **Ted wants to measure the length of a swimming pool. Which unit of measure should he use?**

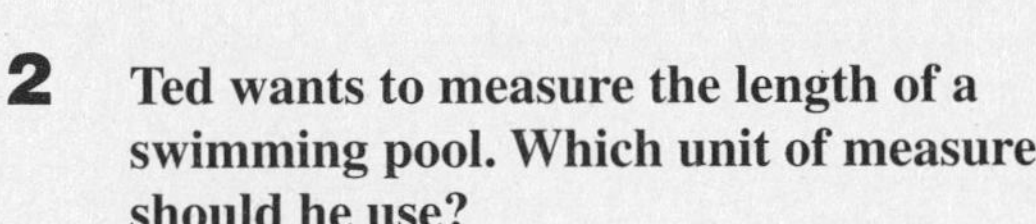

J milliliters
K centimeters
L meters
M kilometers

3 **Jen and her mother drove from their house to Jen's grandmother's house. About how far did they drive if the odometer read 6,437.8 mi when they left and 6,473.9 mi when they arrived?**

A about 25 mi
B about 34 mi
C about 36 mi
D about 41 mi

6,474
− 6,438
36

Sometimes you can tell that one of the answers doesn't make sense. You can eliminate that choice right away.

If the answer you got is not given, go back.

- ★ Check that you answered the right question.
- ★ Check the numbers you copied.
- ★ Check your calculations.

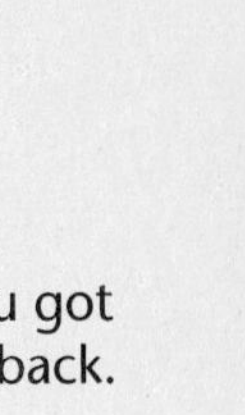

Some multiple-choice questions present information in tables, graphs, or in pictures. To solve the problem, you need to carefully interpret the data. But one thing is always the same–fill out your answer sheet carefully!

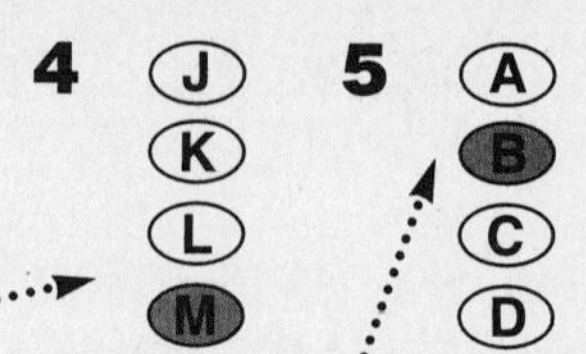

Remember to fill in only one circle for each question on your answer

Make sure that you completely fill in the correct letter for each item. Be careful if you skip items.

You have a job at the public library. Use the table to answer items 4 and 5.

Public Library Week I	
Day	**Hours**
Monday	$3\frac{1}{2}$
Wednesday	$3\frac{3}{4}$
Friday	$4\frac{1}{4}$

4 **How many hours did you work the first week?**

J 9 hours

K $10\frac{1}{2}$ hours

L 11 hours

M $11\frac{1}{2}$ hours

$3\frac{1}{2} = 3\frac{2}{4}$

$3\frac{3}{4} = 3\frac{3}{4}$

$+\ 4\frac{1}{4} = 4\frac{1}{4}$

$10\frac{6}{4} = 11\frac{2}{4} = 11\frac{1}{2}$

Check that you found the correct data in the table.

5 **Your friend Lee worked $5\frac{1}{2}$ hours on Friday. How much longer did she work on that day than you did?**

A 1 hour

B $1\frac{1}{4}$ hours

C $2\frac{1}{4}$ hours

D $2\frac{1}{2}$ hours

$5\frac{1}{2} = 5\frac{2}{4}$

$-\ 4\frac{1}{4} = 4\frac{1}{4}$

$1\frac{1}{4}$

Always check your work for common calculation mistakes.

It's Your Turn: Practicing Multiple-Choice Questions

1 **Luis has $2.45 in change. He has only nickels, dimes and quarters. If he has 1 more dime than he has nickels, and 2 more quarters than dimes, how many of each coin does he have?**

A 6 quarters, 7 dimes, 5 nickels
B 7 quarters, 5 dimes, 4 nickels
C 8 quarters, 4 dimes, 1 nickel
D 9 quarters, 1 dime, 2 nickels

Answer Sheet

1		2		3	
	Ⓐ		Ⓙ		Ⓐ
	Ⓑ		Ⓚ		Ⓑ
	Ⓒ		Ⓛ		Ⓒ
	Ⓓ		Ⓜ		Ⓓ

3 **Maya and her sister are going to a fair. They have $16.50 between them. They use half of their money to buy tickets. Then they buy 2 lemonades and 2 hot dogs.**

Refreshments	
Item	**Cost**
Lemonade	$2.25
Pocorn	$1.50
Hot Dog	$1.75

Check that you used the correct data from the table.

How much money do they have left? Use the prices in the table.

J $0.25
K $1.25
L $1.75
M $2.25

3 **Use your protractor. Find the measure of $\angle A$.**

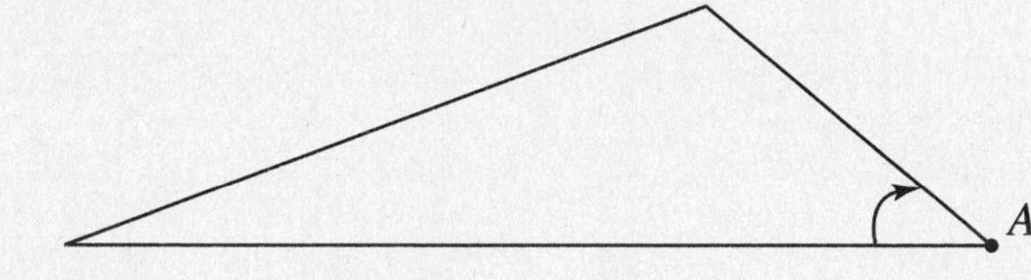

A 20°
B 40°
C 140°
D 160°

ANSWERS: See page 14.

Use Your Own Words: Answering Open-Answer

Some problems in a test are just like other math activities you do—you have to write your own answer on a line or in a space shown. Open-answer questions, or constructed response questions, may ask you to:

★ solve a problem, show your work, and explain how you got your answer.
★ draw a picture, diagram, graph, or table.
★ write a problem.

Suppose you collect the oil from a leaking car for one hour. The amount you collect is about 280 mL.

A **Estimate the amount of oil this car would waste in one year, if it kept leaking at that rate. Write your answer in liters.**

Amount of oil about 2,400 liters

One day = 24 hours
280 x 24: Round 300 x 20 = 6,000 mL
One year = 365 days
365 x 6,000: Round 400 x 6,000 = 2,400,000 mL
= 2,400 L

B **Explain in words the mathematics you used to make your estimate. Include an explanation of how you know your answer is reasonable.**

First I estimated the amount of oil leaked in one day by multiplying 300 x 20. Then I multiplied that product by the numbers of days in a year rounded to the nearest hundreds: 400 x 6,000 = 2,400,000 mL. I divided by 1,000 to change milliliters to liters.

So, what's the plan?

You can use the steps you already know to help you solve any math problem.

READ What question do you need to answer?

PLAN What do you need to do?

SOLVE What steps will you take to solve the problem?

LOOK Does your answer

Always show your work. Even if you make a small error, you may get partial credit if you show you understand how to solve the problem.

Make sure you answer the question!

Test-Taking Hint:

Constructed-response questions are usually worth more points than multiple-choice questions. Plan your time.

It's Your Turn: Practicing Open-Answer Questions

Try these open-answer questions.

1 Melissa earns $12.50 per day at the Paws Pet Grooming shop. She also gets $1.00 for each animal she washes. Melissa works 4 hours a day for 3 days each week. On a typical day, she washes 15 animals. Jamal earns $6.50 per hour at the Squeaky Clean Pet Grooming shop and works 10 hours each week.

A Write an algebraic expression to show how much Melissa earns per day. Explain what any variables represent.

____

____

____

Remember that you are being asked to explain three things. Check that you have answered all questions.

B Evaluate the expression you wrote to find Melissa's earnings for an average day.

____

____

____

C Who earns more each week – Melissa or Jamal? Explain how you got your answer.

____

____

____

ANSWERS: See page 14.

2 Use the spinner and the 1–6 number cube to answer the questions.

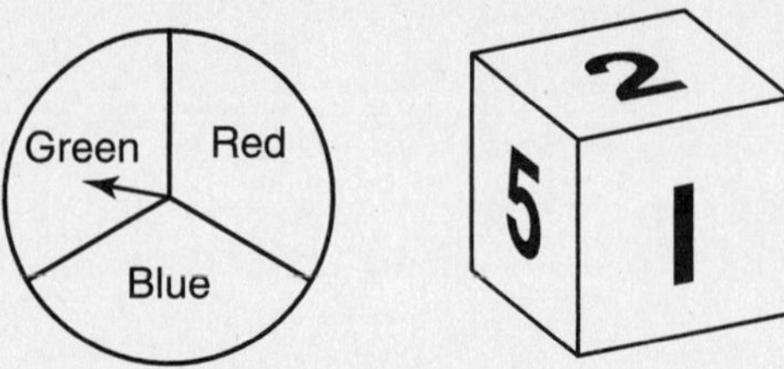

A Draw a tree diagram to represent all possible outcomes of one spin of the spinner and one toss of the number cube.

B Write the probabilities as fractions.

P (green, 2) ____________ *P* (red or green, 1) ____________

P (red, 2) ____________ *P* (blue, less than 3) ____________

P (blue, odd) ____________ *P* (red or blue, even) ____________

C Describe an outcome for each probability.

100% ________________________

$\frac{2}{9}$ ________________________

✓ Check, please ✓

Before turning in a test, go back one last time to check.

- ☐ I understood and answered the questions asked.
- ☐ I checked my calculations for errors.
- ☐ My answers make sense.

ANSWERS: See page 14.

Test-Takers' Handbook: Answers

Here are the answers to the practice items you tried in the Test-Takers' Handbook.

Page 87: **1** B **2** J **3** B

Page 89: Answers may vary. A good answer will:

A $12.50 + $1($n$) = E
E = earnings, and n = the number of animals Melissa washes.

B When n = 15:
$12.50 + ($1.00 x 15) = E; $12.50 + $15 = $27.50
Melissa earns $27.50 on an average day.

C Melissa: $27.50 × 3 = $82.50; Jamal: $6.50 × 10 = $65.00
$82.50 > $65.00, so Melissa earns more than Jamal each week.

Page 90: A

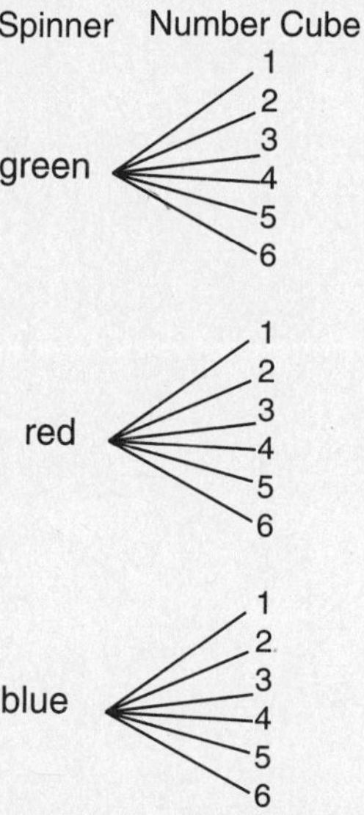

B P (green, 2) = $\frac{1}{18}$ P (red or green, 1) = $\frac{2}{18} = \frac{1}{9}$
P (red, 6) = $\frac{1}{18}$ P (blue, less than 3 = $\frac{2}{18} = \frac{1}{9}$
P (blue, odd) = $\frac{3}{18} = \frac{1}{6}$ P (red or blue, even) = $\frac{6}{18} = \frac{1}{3}$

C Answers may vary. Possible answers are given.
100%: red, blue, or green; 1, 2, 3, 4, 5, or 6
$\frac{2}{9}$: (blue or green, 2 or 4)